IT
WAS
A
DIFFERENT
GAME
The
Elmer
Layden
Story

IT
WAS
A
DIFFERENT
GAME

**The
Elmer
Layden
Story**

●

ELMER LAYDEN
with
Ed Snyder

PRENTICE-HALL, INC., ENGLEWOOD CLIFFS, N.J.

IT WAS A DIFFERENT GAME: The Elmer Layden Story
by Elmer Layden with Ed Snyder
© 1969 by Elmer Layden and Ed Snyder
13-507517-3
Library of Congress Catalog Card Number: 74-81969
Printed in the United States of America   ·   T
Prentice-Hall International, Inc., London
Prentice-Hall of Australia, Pty. Ltd., Sydney
Prentice-Hall of Canada, Ltd., Toronto
Prentice-Hall of India Private Ltd., New Delhi
Prentice-Hall of Japan, Inc., Tokyo
Fourth printing...... November, 1969

Introduction

On a chill, dank afternoon 45 years ago, Elmer Layden climbed up on a horse for me and saved my life by not falling off.

Knute Rockne's reaction at seeing the fullback and three other members of his first string backfield astride uncurried refugees from a South Bend ice and coal company was menacing. But with the Princeton game only five days away, it most surely would have become uncontrollable had any one of the famous Four Horsemen slipped out of the saddle and jammed up an arm or a leg.

None of the Horsemen were real horsemen, of course, but they all rode successfully down life's highway, and I had the privilege of riding with Layden over a few of the hurdles that loomed up on the course late in the canter, when he was commissioner of professional football.

It was a different game then. Athletes had not yet become professional entertainers, and millionaires could be found only on a yacht or in the rotogravure. Locker rooms were the exclusive domain of dedicated workmen who learned the signals before they memorized stock tables and pension formulas.

It was a different game in college in Layden's day, too, and if you care to argue that it was better, I may have to agree. At any rate, it merits accurate retelling for the record and no one is better qualified to tell it than Layden, who is not unmindful nor unappreciative of the need for the preservation of some old-time values.

George Strickler
Sports Editor
Chicago *Tribune*

Preface

My grandson, Elmer Layden III, plays football in grammar school. The first day he went out for the team, his coach told him, "You know your grandfather was one of the Four Horsemen of Notre Dame."

Little Elmer said nothing, but when he got home, he asked his mother, "Mom, what's a Horseman of Notre Dame?"

Many, many years earlier, his father, Elmer Jr., also played on a grammar school football team. One day, between quarters, he came to the sidelines, and I, as a dutiful father, gave him this advice: "Keep your head up, son, when you're running with the ball. They have holes in their secondary, and you could make some long gains if you looked where you were going."

Elmer Jr., then in seventh grade, replied: "Thanks, Dad, but they don't play football that way any more."

This is why I think it's time to tell sons and grandsons that football was played in the 1920's, even if it was not as sophisticated as today's game; that Notre Dame did have Four Horsemen; that those of us who played and coached the game in those "dark ages" considered football a sport more than a business, and that a lot of us had a lot of fun.

Elmer Layden

Acknowledgments

The authors are indebted to a number of persons who helped piece together reminiscences and provide background. Among those who took the time and trouble to help out are George Strickler, Tippy Dye, Joe Petritz, Bob Cahill, Chet Grant, Brue Jackson, George Halas, Art Rooney, John Ladner, the Public Relations Department of Loras College in Dubuque, Iowa, Clair Brown and Eileen Mauro of Duquesne University's Public Relations Department.

Nor can we forget Henry Wurzer for his encouragement; John O'Toole, who served as our lawyer in this venture; Fran Block, who typed much of the manuscript, and John Walker, who read the final proof.

Our thanks to Edythe Layden, Mrs. Joan Layden Jones and Mrs. Dorie Layden for rummaging through clippings and photographs from the past, and to Pat Snyder who helped catalog them as well as type some of the chapters.

IT
WAS
A
DIFFERENT
GAME
The
Elmer
Layden
Story

CHAPTER ONE

One October day in 1924, I was launched toward the College Football Hall of Fame along with Harry Stuhldreher, Jim Crowley, and Don Miller. That was the day we played Army at the Polo Grounds in New York City, and Grantland Rice named us the Four Horsemen of Notre Dame. The 1920's often have been called the Golden Age of Sports, and certainly it was a golden age of sports writing as shown by the way Granny Rice began that story:

"Outlined against a blue-gray October sky, the Four Horsemen rode again.

"In dramatic lore they are known as famine, pestilence, destruction and death. These are only aliases. Their real names are: Stuhldreher, Miller, Crowley and Layden. They formed the crest of the South Bend cyclone before which another fighting Army team was swept over the precipice at the Polo Grounds this afternoon as 55,000 spectators peered down upon the bewildering panorama spread out on the green plain below."

Since we only beat Army by a score of 13-7, you may wonder what stirred such a burst of thundering prose. Now that forty-five years have passed, I think the truth can safely be told. The fellow behind the Four Horsemen idea was our student publicity man, George Strickler, who now is sports editor of the *Chicago Tribune*.

Over the twenty-five years I spent in football and in the years since, George has been one of my closest friends. He was publicity director of the National Football League during the five years I was commissioner, and we relive those times at regular intervals over a drink or a dinner.

George grew up on the Notre Dame campus where his father ran the university's slaughterhouse. In those days, Notre Dame raised its own food. Naturally, when he reached college age, George went to Notre Dame and, as all young men of that era, needed a job of some kind to pay his way.

The fabled Knute Rockne was Notre Dame's athletic director, head football coach and track coach. Among his many friendships, Rock had developed a close rapport with the local outlets of both Western Union and Postal Telegraph which enabled him to have an athletic publicity man of his own choosing at no cost either to the university or to himself. The lucky student chosen for this job lived off space rates paid by the leading newspapers and wire services for stories about Notre Dame practice sessions between games. These stories moved over the telegraph wires, and if some maverick student tried

2

to bootleg a story behind the publicity man's back, Rock was in a position to shut him off at the telegraph key. This protected the student press agent from interlopers and assured the boy of all the income he could drum up from newspapers and wire services that wanted to keep posted on Notre Dame football.

They say Arch Ward, who later became a famous sports editor of the *Chicago Tribune*, was the astute student who first brought this idea of managed news to Rock's attention. He was the first person to hold the job, whose only drawback came when the team took a trip. We traveled, of course, by Pullman car and where you slept pretty much indicated your status. The starters had lower berths; the substitutes the upper berths. The publicity man and the trainer had to sleep on the floor under one of the lower berths.

George Strickler became Rock's publicity man in 1924. On the side he was a dedicated movie fan and admits to seeing one epic of that era at least six times. It was titled: "The Four Horsemen of the Apocalypse."

The night before our team embarked for New York to play Army, Strickler saw the picture one more time, and visions of famine, pestilence, destruction, and death must have galloped through his dreams as he slept under a lower berth on our way there.

At half time, as Strickler recalls it, he stepped out into the aisle of the press box and began chatting with four sportswriters gathered there. George told them that the way our backfield ran over Army in the first half reminded him of the Four Horsemen of the Apocalypse. One of the writers was Granny Rice, and next morning

3

Harry, Jimmy, Don, and I woke up as not just another Notre Dame backfield, but the Four Horsemen of Notre Dame.

Some years later, George ran across one of the other writers who had listened to his idea, and asked, "What would have happened if all four of you had gone for that Four Horseman idea?"

Having coined the name and successfully planted it, George was not about to sit back. Right after we got back to the campus the following Monday, he rounded up four horses from a livery stable, got us dressed in our football suits and took our picture. Then he merchandised them around the country. As recently as 1964, I ran across the same picture in a national magazine. It was in an advertisement by the New England Mutual Life Insurance Company that made a big point of the fact that forty years had passed since George put us on horseback.

I sometimes wonder how I'd have spent those years if George's idea had fallen flat? I wonder if I'd have gone into coaching or stuck with my original ambition of practicing law? I wonder if all of us connected with that single football game in 1924 would have grown as close as we did over the years that followed. Certainly it was the closeness that developed, not only among the four of us, but among all of the players on the 1924 squad, that was the biggest dividend we earned from George Strickler's great idea. One thing for sure, everybody connected with the game collected dividends: our coach, our teammates and even Granny Rice.

Rock probably had much better backfields than us in his coaching days (I suspect his 1930 crowd was) but he

4

never had one that was better known nor, for that matter, lighter. Even by 1924 standards, we were small. By today's standards, we were almost midgets. We'd probably have trouble getting on most of today's college teams as student managers.

A week after the Army game, we went East again to play Princeton and worked out the day before at a country club in New Jersey that had an old potato scales back of the clubhouse. After practice, we weighed ourselves. Harry weighed 158 pounds; Jim and Don both were 164. I was 162.

Now that I've reached age sixty-five, I flatter quite easily, and nothing flatters me more than meeting someone for the first time who will remark: "Oh, you certainly must have lost weight since your days as one of the Four Horsemen!" I smile my most modest smile and respond: "Thanks a lot, but I'm actually almost twenty pounds heavier."

At what seems like hundreds of football banquets I've attended, it always happens that one of the linemen on that 1924 team follows me to the microphone and explains quite casually that without the Seven Mules* opening "those big holes," the Four Horsemen would have been just another four nags. Rip Miller, who played tackle on the team and has spent almost a lifetime in one athletic capacity or another at the U.S. Naval Academy, is particularly good with this needle. Well, one night, they made the mistake of introducing Rip first and, of

---

* Ed Hunsinger and Chuck Collins were the ends; Joe Bach and Rip Miller the tackles; Noble Kizer and John Weibel the guards, and Adam Walsh the center.

5

course, he told of all the big holes that our line made for us. Then it was my turn. "When I started playing behind the Seven Mules in 1922," I began, "I was 5 feet 10 inches tall and weighed 169 pounds. Three years later, when I finished, I was 5 feet, 11½ inches tall and weighed 162 pounds, so those holes couldn't have been that big."

The name Seven Mules came from Adam Walsh, our captain. He was understandably fed up hearing about the Four Horsemen by the end of the 1924 season. On the way to the Rose Bowl game, our train stopped in some western town for water and a group of people gathered and called for the Four Horsemen. Adam stepped out of the car, called the rest of the line and said, "You're looking at the best part of the team, the Seven Mules."

Adam really was the hero of the 1924 Army game. He was the center and played the game with broken bones in both hands. For a tackle or a guard, this would have been quite a feat; for a center, it was heroic. What made it more courageous was the fact that Adam played opposite one of the great all-time Army football players, Edgar Garbisch. Ed Garbisch had been an All-American at Washington and Jefferson before he entered West Point and was one of the real football heroes of that era. Some say he was the first roving linebacker, jumping in and out of the line when Army was on defense. The fact that Adam could handle him, let alone handle him with two broken hands, still stands as one of the great performances in Notre Dame's football history.

As the years wore on, Granny Rice became almost a member of our team. None of us spent any time in New York without looking him up and spending a delightful interlude with a man who not only was a great writer, but also a magnificent storyteller. On the 25th anniversary of his story about the Four Horsemen, we gave him a testimonial dinner, as well we should since without his story we would have been just another backfield. And when he died in 1954, we served as honorary pallbearers. I have been to many sports gatherings in my life, but none that topped Granny's funeral for the array of sports celebrities, past and present, that turned out to pay him final tribute.

Of course the closest ties forged by Granny's story were between Harry, Jim, Don, and me. We began to think of ourselves not as individuals, but as musketeers who were one for all and all for one. This spirit carried on for years afterwards, until Harry died in 1965 leaving us without a quarterback in every sense of the word. For Harry not only called the signals in our playing days, he also kept calling them in the years that followed. He stage-managed our debut in the hectic days of professional football that marked the mid-1920's, a subject you'll hear about later. After he left coaching, he joined United States Steel Corporation, traveled around the country all year long giving speeches, and staged a family reunion with one or the other or all of us at regular and irregular intervals. We grew closer together, I feel, than most brothers do and all thanks to Harry.

I'm sorry he wasn't around in the fall of 1967 to see the Peter Arno cartoon that appeared in the *New Yorker* magazine. It showed four football players running together with one letting a pass slip through his hands. The coach on the sideline was saying: "There they go,

7

the Four Horsemen—Famine, Pestilence, Death and Butterfingers."

I wonder which one of us Harry would have called Butterfingers?

CHAPTER TWO

I still marvel at how I managed to stay at Notre Dame long enough to become one of the Four Horsemen. When I arrived, I was one sick kid, and I was still sick a year later when the Four Horsemen were put together as a unit for the first time. My illness was that most dreadful sickness of all—homesickness. I've heard stories later of youngsters being homesick, but I maintain that I hold the record for the longest case of homesickness ever suffered by one person.

Home was a frame house on Kirkwood Boulevard in Davenport, Iowa. Home was a sports fan of a dad named Tom Layden and a dear of a mother who was Rosemary Bartemeyer before she married dad. Home was an older brother, Clarence, whom the kids at school called "Irish," two sisters, Elizabeth and Catherine, and a kid brother who had been christened Francis Louis Layden. He was ten years my junior and when he was born, my older brother and I visited mother in the hospital. In that era, hospitals weren't so fussy about letting youngsters inside. Clarence, my elder by five years, marched into the room and told mother, "I don't care what you name the baby, we're going to call him Mike." And to this day, fifty-five years later, Francis Louis Layden is still called "Mike." He turned up later as a player—something of a problem to me when I arrived as Notre Dame's coach.

Living on a boulevard, we had a lovely strip of grass down the center for playing ball. Since automobiles were not much of a problem in those years before World War I, there was a ball game of some kind, football or baseball, going on most of the time on this piece of public lawn. As in every neighborhood in every town at every time, there was an old lady on the block who could not stand kids, particularly noisy kids. In our case, the widow in question was a most religious person who not only could not abide us, but particularly could not abide our playing ball in the boulevard on Sundays. One Sunday she finally lost patience and called the police. They arrived with a paddy wagon and hauled Clarence and me and the others off to jail. They even put us in a cell. About that time, my uncle, who was a detective on the force, arrived and we were sprung forthwith. And that might be the story of my home town—there was always a relative of some kind who could be of help in a pinch. My grandfather Bartemeyer was on the board of directors of a local bank and that didn't hurt either.

We had an old upright piano in the front parlor— remember when the living room was the front parlor?

My sisters went to a convent-type high school and were encouraged to take music. My mother asked me if I'd like to study the piano with them. I said, "No, I'd rather play baseball."

As grammar school kids, we all went to Sacred Heart School. After that, the girls went to a Catholic girls' high school, but Clarence and I were sent to Davenport High, a free public school. I can't remember that either of us set any records as students, but the two of us along with two other boys, Ike Sears and Davenport Day, once set a high school record for the half-mile relay in the famous Drake Relays at Des Moines. Of course, we played every sport the high school offered, which then consisted of football, basketball, and track. In these activities, we were versatile, if nothing else. Take the track team: I ran the 100 and 220 yard dashes, the 110 and 220 yard hurdles, and participated in the shot put, broad jump, and high jump. A friendly historian in later years once described me as a one-man track team. Basketball then still featured the center jump after each score. The stress was on defense and I was a standing guard, a fixture soon to be made obsolete in basketball. We won one major game by the astonishingly low score of 11-9. I recall we rolled up our biggest score in a 21-20 victory during a state tournament, beating Springville for the title. If anything, basketball was just football without pads. The caliber of basketball players in my area was such that I was named to the All-State high school team one year.

I never went on to become much of a basketball player, even though I kept playing at the sport through college and even coached it for a couple of years. Basketball

11

just seemed a way of keeping your wind up between football season and track season. All I ever really got from it was a bad knee.

My debut as a high school football player was not exactly easy. As I was small, the coach did not want to give me a uniform. Finally the sports editor of the Davenport newspaper, who happened to be a cousin, talked him into giving me a tryout, and I eventually justified this editor's confidence by becoming All-State quarterback in my senior year, 1920.

High school football stars did not then have the joy of picking college offers that they have today. I had only one tentative offer of a football scholarship and that was from the University of Iowa. My dad was a rabid Iowa fan; in fact he later was made an honorary member of a fraternity at Iowa because he was such an ardent rooter. The Iowa people, however, found out about my bad knee and their interest soon waned. Meanwhile, my old high school coach, Walter Halas, had moved to Notre Dame as head baseball and basketball coach as well as assistant to Rockne in coaching football and track. Walter, who was the older brother of the George Halas of Chicago Bears' fame, had left Davenport High after my junior year so he was less impressed than he might have been by my football prowess. He did remember me as a good basketball player and a versatile trackman. Late in the summer of 1921, when he was on a visit to Davenport, he offered me a scholarship to Notre Dame—room, board, and tuition in exchange for a part-time job and going out for every sport. That was my one and only solid offer of a college education in return for doing what I enjoyed most; playing sports.

With a stiff upper lip, I left Davenport for South Bend, Indiana, which I quite soon found not to my liking. I arrived to find that I was rooming with two senior members of the football team in a basement dormitory near the university dining hall where we earned our keep three times a day as waiters. The room contained one double-decker bunk and a cot. To permit sightly more freedom of movement, my two upper-class roommates had perched the cot on top of the double-decker bunk. "That is your bed," I was told. Well, I climbed up to try it out and immediately discovered if I rolled one way I'd fall about 12 feet; if I rolled the other way I'd scorch myself on the steam pipes running along the ceiling. At that, I picked up my suitcase and marched over to Badin Hall, a student dormitory where I had a tuition-paying cousin from Fort Wayne, Indiana. He let me sleep on his floor for the first two weeks I was at Notre Dame. At least I had nowhere to fall nor any hot steam pipes.

Before those two weeks were up, I talked my cousin into taking me downtown to see the railroad station. I was in the midst of looking up timetables for trains back to Davenport when Danny Coughlin, a member of the football squad, came along and invited us to come to football practice. His timely appearance settled me down for a week or so.

When my cousin detected the next bout of severe homesickness, he walked me down to Walter Halas' home and Walter tried to pep talk me into staying. As a last resort, he brought Knute Rockne over. Rock, in his best selling way said, "Son, we've never lost a freshman from our team yet." To this, I thought, "Mr. Rockne, your record is about to be broken."

Yes, I went home. More than once, too. So often that my subconscious has erased the exact number of times from my memory. I'd arrive in Davenport and mope around the house for a few days. Nobody scolded me. My dad made it plain every time that I did not have to go back to college. Finally I'd muster up enough nerve and go back only to keep making collect calls homeward for more encouragement to stay put.

You might imagine that by the end of my freshman year, I would have been thoroughly cured. I wasn't. However, I did get better. I tell friends I only quit school five times as a sophomore, which really is an exaggeration. However, a new complication had arisen.

During the summer at home, I'd become quite friendly with a young Davenport lady who was going to the University of Wisconsin. When school resumed, my heart was not so much yearning for Davenport as for Madison, Wisconsin. On top of this, I was not getting to play much football. Rock had decided I should be a halfback and the team had plenty of good halfbacks. So when the first waves of homesickness swept over me, I began yearning for a change of college scenery and took preliminary steps to try and get an athletic scholarship at the University of Wisconsin. I figured I'd at least be near the young lady from Davenport even if I didn't get to play as much football as I liked.

Once my transfer negotiations were under way, I felt courageous enough to bring up the subject of my constant bench-sitting to Coach Rockne. To my surprise, he not only listened to my complaint, but replied, "All right, Layden, I'll let you start the next game." That next game of the 1922 season was with Army. It was to be the last Army-Notre Dame game played on the Plains at West Point. As I remember, it also was the last time that an Army-Notre Dame game was by invitation only. I couldn't miss this one, so I put aside my plans of transferring to Wisconsin and, as things worked out, never seriously considered them again.

The Army-Notre Dame series began in 1913. Jesse Harper, who was Notre Dame's coach and athletic director at that time, scheduled the first game with the help of Bill Cotter, a Notre Dame alumnus. Army had been playing Yale on the date scheduled—a Saturday late in November—and neither team found it to be a good arrangement, so the story goes. It seems that both teams got so beat up that neither Army nor Yale was in fit condition to meet their traditional rivals—Navy and Harvard—later in the season. Harper managed to talk Army out of a $1,000 guarantee to bring his team to West Point, and it's been told that Notre Dame made a profit of only $5 from the game. Yet it did far more in the long run; it put Notre Dame on the map as a football power and launched a series that ran uninterrupted through 1947.

Notre Dame won that first game, 35-13, and brought to national attention the power of the forward pass. Gus Dorais was the passer; Knute Rockne the receiver. It was Dorais to Rockne passes that beat Army and put the spotlight on the tactical advantages of passing. In later years, it often has been said that Dorais and Rockne invented the forward pass. No, they didn't invent it; they perfected it and turned football from a grunt and grind ground game into a more open game.

By 1922, the Army game had become a traditional rivalry and reached a popularity that outgrew the temporary bleachers on the Plains of West Point. As I recall, admittance to the game was by invitation and the guests caused a part of the bleachers to collapse during that 1922 game. The West Point folks looked forward to hosting the Notre Dame team. We would arrive on Friday morning, work out, eat our meals in the cadet dining hall, and spend the night at an old inn on the academy grounds. On Friday nights, Rock would gather with the West Point friends and regale them with his wit and personality. The biggest jolt came on Saturday morning at six o'clock. The Army fired a cannon to signal reveille, and when this gun boomed off, it almost blew me out of bed. The old inn where we stayed shook from the reverberation of the blast.

Like every coach, Rock had his superstitions, and one was that his team should enter and leave the West Point dining hall by a side door. I don't know if this really was a superstition. He just might have been afraid his team would be trampled to death by the marching cadets if it entered the front door. At any rate, it had no salutary effect on the outcome of the game, which ended in a scoreless tie.

This was our seventh game of the 1922 season. Until that tie, we had a perfect record, beating Kalamazoo,

St. Louis, Purdue, DePauw, Georgia Tech, and Indiana.

Our next game was with Butler, and out of it came my lucky break, or rather a most unlucky broken leg for our regular fullback, Paul Castner. Paul was out for the rest of the season. Rock came up and said, "Layden, I want you to try out for fullback." I replied that we had two other fullbacks, Bill Cerney and Bernie Livergood, both of whom weighed more than I did. "Never mind," Rockne said, "I need a small fullback because our line opens small holes."

CHAPTER THREE

My debut as a fullback was less than spectacular. It came a week later against Carnegie Tech, and while I did not distinguish myself, it was the first time that the Four Horsemen played together as a unit.

Before reporting what happened, I should tell a little bit about the way Rockne operated and the football climate in which he had to operate. First of all, the platoon system we know today did not exist. The rules on substitution prevented any player from returning to the game in the same quarter he was taken out. This rule continued, by the way, until the late 1940's when platooning was first introduced into the college game. Later it was revoked and then reinstated. Before platooning, your college football player had to know defense as well as offense; he had to tackle as well as block, and, in my opinion, was the better for it.

Rock was a great student of the game and the rules of the game. He had a lawyer's insight into the interpretation of the rules and his introduction of the so-called Notre Dame shift early in the 1920's sent the rules committee back into session looking for loopholes to plug. Rock, of course, did not invent the shift. Amos Alonzo Stagg came up with the idea years earlier at the University of Chicago and Jesse Harper brought it along to Notre Dame. Like the forward pass, Rock didn't invent it, he refined it. In the first version of his shift, the ball was snapped at the instant the backfield stopped shifting, which meant that while their feet were set, their bodies had forward momentum. The rulesmakers plugged this loophole by insisting that the backs not only bring their feet to a set position, but also have no forward motion before the ball was centered. Rock then taught his backfield how to twist their bodies while their feet were set. This gave not only the impression of motion, but also a certain momentum to their takeoff at the snap. Back went the rules committee and out came a ruling that required backs to come to a full stop; feet, body and all, for one second.

One of the vigorous opponents of Rock's shift, though they were good friends, was Bob Zuppke, the famous Illinois coach. For years Zup liked to tell of his first visit to the Notre Dame campus. In his thick Dutch accent, he'd say, "First I go to the football field and the whole team is shifting . . . hike, one, two. Then I walk around the campus and the whole student body is shifting . . . hike, one, two. Then I go to see the president of the school and he's shifting . . . hike, one, two . . . and, do you know, he was the only one doing it legally."

With his gift of improvisation, Rock also came up with his own brand of platooning. He turned what might have been called his second team into what he called his "shock troops." He would often start the first half of a game playing the "shock troops" with the idea of wearing down an opponent while his first team stayed fresh and while he studied the opposition. The idea was a good one and copied in later years by many other coaches.

Jim Crowley and Don Miller had been playing with the first team. Harry Stuhldreher also had put in some first team time as quarterback. Against Carnegie Tech, I was to join this august group for the first time and become the Fourth Horseman. Lots of our backfield teammates later called themselves "The Fifth Horseman."

Rock started the "shock troops" against Carnegie Tech and they worked the ball down to the 5-yard line. Rock called Harry and me over to him and said, "I'm sending you in." Thinking it was fourth down, he gave Harry a pass play to call. I was to be the receiver. In we went and Harry immediately discovered that it was only third down. Now in those days we did not huddle; the huddle still was several years away. Harry called signals from behind the center in our basic "T" formation, then we shifted and the play was under way. Harry decided since it was third down, he wouldn't pass, but rather send me on a fullback buck into the line. As he called this signal, and we shifted, I sensed this change in plans at the split second Bob Reagan centered me the ball. The ball

21

bounced off my knee, sailed five yards forward and landed on the goal line where our end, George Vergara, fell on it for a touchdown. Now you know why I can tell my grandchildren I had a hand in scoring a touchdown the first time I played with the Four Horsemen. Or should I say a knee?

When I used to tell this story at football banquets, I would say, "It certainly sounds like one heckuva great trick play, but Rock put it back in the bag and never used it anymore."

In spite of its somewhat confused fullback, Notre Dame beat Carnegie Tech, 26-0, and finished the 1922 season by losing to Nebraska. Nebraska upset us in 1923, and again this was our only loss of the season. By this time, I was playing regularly on the first team with Harry, Jim, and Don. We played Army that year at Ebbetts Field in Brooklyn to a capacity house of 30,000. Granny Rice covered that game and wrote in his memoirs that it was the first time he saw the Four Horsemen play together as a unit. His nickname for us was still a year away.

During the winter, I kept in shape as a member of the Notre Dame basketball team. Come spring, I ran with the track team, which also was coached by Rockne. My best event was the 100-yard dash, and at one point I held the Indiana college record. However, I never managed to please the coach with my style of sprinting. "You dig the first 60 yards, then go into your 'float' for the next 20, then sprint the last 20," he'd tell me. By "float," Rock meant that your momentum would carry you these middle 20 yards. For some reason, I never could "float" the way he wanted. Whenever I tried, I'd get beat. Not that I wasn't beaten other times, digging the full 100 yards.

The great sprinter of that era was Charlie Paddock. One year at the famous Drake Relays in Des Moines, Iowa, they arranged a special handicap race at 100 yards for Charlie. I got a 5-yard head start. Against Charlie, even that didn't help.

A good sprinter in the 1920's had to be part gopher. Sprinters today race from what are called starting blocks. In my time, he dug holes for himself in the cinder track in which he planted his feet to push off. After an afternoon of entering qualifying heats at a major relay event, a sprinter could be almost as tired from digging as he was from running.

I was glad for the 1924 football season to start because, by now, the Four Horsemen had played together long enough to know how to act together as a backfield. By the standards of that day, we had a tough schedule in 1924. And here it seems time to tell about the way the smart coaches of the 1920's scheduled their football games.

In a book that was published in 1925, Rock devoted a whole chapter to the art of scheduling games. His advice can be summed up by this statement: Have two breathers before every tough game. Since most teams played a nine-game schedule, this meant three tough games a season and six breathers.

I'm sure coaches today would love to have the same flexibility in making schedules that their famous predecessors had. As I write this book, I'm looking over the 1969 Notre Dame football schedule and I can't find a breather in the ten games. Moreover, I expect that this schedule was completed at least six years ago, if not sooner, and, if it was, the present Notre Dame coach, Ara Parseghian, wasn't even on the scene yet. He was still coaching at Northwestern. And speaking of Northwestern, Tippy Dye, their athletic director, tells me that he is scheduling games twelve years from now.

During Rock's time, you scheduled games almost on a year to year basis. You seldom were caught opening with a team you couldn't beat. During the first three years I was at Notre Dame, we opened against Kalamazoo College from Kalamazoo, Michigan. I wonder if Kazoo, as we called it, still plays football? If it does, it certainly doesn't open the season against any Notre Dame. (Parenthetically, I might say that I have heard that Kalamazoo has great college baseball teams. It may surprise you that the big sport at Notre Dame until the Rockne era was baseball.)

We opened the 1924 season against Lombard, located in Galesburg, Illinois. We won, 40-0. The second week, we took on Wabash and won 34-0. Then we played Army and became Four Horsemen. By now, the Army game had been moved to the Polo Grounds and this time we had another capacity crowd, only bigger than in Brooklyn, 55,000. After that, the Army game moved to Yankee Stadium, where it remained through 1946. The House that Babe Ruth Built, as they called Yankee Stadium, had even a greater capacity and Notre Dame filled the place every time it played the Army there. It was blessed with what became known as subway alumni, and when the Fighting Irish came to town, they rode the subways up to the Bronx and appeared in record numbers at the box office. Even in the depths of the Great Depression, the subway alumni filled Yankee Stadium for the Army-Notre Dame game and contributed heavily to the athletic funds of both schools. Army, of course, was sure of a sell-out against Navy. Notre Dame, in those days, looked to the Army game for a sure sell-out. The game was moved away from Yankee Stadium only once until 1947 when the series came to a temporary close with a game at South Bend. The one transfer of site was in 1930, Rock's last season, when the game was played in Chicago's Soldier Field and drew 110,000 people who sat through a driving rain to see Notre Dame pull one out of the fire with three minutes to go, 7-6.

Fresh from becoming Four Horsemen, we went back East to play Princeton and pulled off what then was called the "perfect play." Before I tell you about this perfect play, I should review one of the rules of that era. Today when the ball is downed out-of-bounds or near the sideline, the ball is moved out to a point 15 yards from the sideline. In 1924, you played the ball where it was downed and this could be just inches from the sideline. However, when the ball was carried out-of-bounds, it was moved to the center of the field, not 15 yards from the sideline. Our so-called perfect play originated from a point just a few feet from the sideline. All of our linemen were to the left of our center whose feet when he bent over the ball almost touched the sideline. The ball was centered to Harry and in a picture that was taken from the press box, each player carried out his blocking assignment perfectly. That's how the play became known as a perfect play. You would

25

imagine that Harry scored a touchdown under these circumstances. Actually, he went forward only a few yards and stepped out-of-bounds so he could get the ball back in the middle of the field. Field position to a quarterback in those days meant not only what yard line he was on, but also where he was in connection with the side lines.

Field position also dictated strategy. It was considered darn near sinful to attempt a forward pass unless you were inside your opponent's 40-yard line because of the danger of an interception. In the 1923 Army game, Harry threw a pass from our own 40-yard line. The referee of that game was the famous Walter Eckersall. After the game, I rode back to the hotel in a cab with Eckersall and Rock, and Eckersall brought up this pass play. "How could you let a quarterback get away with passing from his own 40?" Eckersall asked Rock. "Imagination . . . imagination . . ." replied Rock as he twirled a cigar in his fingers. While that's what he told Eckersall, you can bet he brought up this breach of good quarterback manners to Harry. You just didn't take that kind of chance in those days.

After Princeton, we took on Georgia Tech for our annual home-coming game. Our home stadium was Cartier Field, which had a wooden bleacher capacity of 22,000. We filled the stands for the Georgia Tech game and won, 34 to 3, giving Notre Dame the 200th victory of a football history that dated back to 1887 when the schedule consisted of one game. Notre Dame played Michigan and lost, 8-0, that year.

We polished off Wisconsin next and finally managed to beat Nebraska the following week. Our next to last game was against Northwestern. As often happened before and since, Notre Dame went into the game a heavy favorite and was lucky to get out alive. Northwestern had a great halfback named Moon Baker, who was one of the finest drop kickers ever to show up on a football field. The game was played in Grant Park Stadium in Chicago, a forerunner to today's Soldier Field. Before we knew it, Baker had kicked two field goals and Northwestern was leading 6-0. Stuhldreher scored in the second quarter, Crowley kicked the extra point and we hung onto this slim lead until late in the fourth period. Then I had one of my brighter moments. Baker passed from deep in his own territory and I intercepted on the Northwestern 40 and managed to slog through the mud for a touchdown. The game ended, 13-6, and all of us breathed a sigh of relief.

I sat out our final game with an injury and nobody missed me as the team pounded Carnegie Tech, 40-19, to bring Rock an undefeated season and what then was called the undisputed championship of the East. Stanford was named champion of the West.

The stage now was set for a showdown to decide the national championship.

Meanwhile, the various all-American teams were chosen and three of the Four Horsemen were fortunate to be named to several first team backfields. Don Miller was the unlucky one among us. A fellow named Red Grange was playing that season for Illinois and he was everybody's unanimous pick for halfback.

CHAPTER FOUR

The 1924 team still holds one Notre Dame record: it was the first and, to date, only Notre Dame team ever to play in a Rose Bowl game. In all fairness to the teams that followed, I have to point out that, since then Notre Dame has had a policy of not playing post-season games. If the National Collegiate Athletic Association ever devises a scheme for a post-season playoff to determine the national collegiate football champion, I would bet Notre Dame will change that policy.

Our Rose Bowl opponent was Stanford, which also had gone through the 1924 season undefeated and was being hailed as champion of the West. Stanford's star player was the great fullback, Ernie Nevers, who later added to his fame as both a professional player and coach of the Chicago Cardinals pro team. The Stanford coach was Glenn "Pop" Warner. Nobody can write a history of the golden age of football without including Pop Warner along with Rock, Zuppke, Amos Alonzo Stagg, and Fielding Yost. These were the five big names; all personalities, all men who brought new ideas to the game.

Before we get to the Rose Bowl, let me tell you about the round-about trip Notre Dame took to the game.

Our team started to Pasadena via New Orleans, slightly south and east of our ultimate destination. Rock felt we needed to get used to warm weather before we got to California, so he plotted what then amounted to a Cook's tour of the Southern half of this country. New Orleans welcomed us with open arms. Tulane University offered its stadium for practice sessions. Loyola of the South treated us to a lunch that began with oysters and went through a sumptuous lineup of Bayou dishes. By the time we got to practice, none of us could run. Rock was not very happy.

Our home base was the Palace Hotel where Rock had decreed a ten o'clock curfew. At eleven, one night, he found Ed Hunsinger and Johnny Weibel in the lobby. They had been out looking for post cards to send to their friends and relatives, but Rock would hear no excuses. He told them to pack up; he was sending them home. Adam Walsh, the team captain, pleaded for mercy the next day and Rock relented.

Our next stop on the way West was Houston, Texas, where Rice Institute had offered us a practice field, and a lot of east Texans offered their hospitality. We spent Christmas in Houston and also held our first pre-Rose Bowl scrimmage. During that scrimmage, I was kicked in the jaw. They hauled me off for x-rays to find that I didn't have a broken jaw, but an abscessed tooth.

When the train pulled out of Houston, Rock canceled our next scheduled stop: El Paso. He decided we had been wined and dined enough and pushed us on to Tucson, Arizona, where the Downtown Quarterback Club of that city had arranged to let us practice at the University of Arizona's football field. By now, my jaw really was sore, so my first stop was at a Tucson dentist, who extracted the sore tooth and scraped the jaw bone.

Slip Madigan met us in Tucson. Slip, a Notre Dame protégé of Rock, was coaching St. Mary's in California and had scouted Stanford for us. He spotted a particular pass play Stanford tried and he explained it in detail. I can best describe it as the forerunner of what today they call the screen pass. Let me say we were ready and Slip's scouting paid off. Now on to the game.

The game was played at Pasadena on January 1, 1925, in what is now called the Rose Bowl, but then was a horse-shoe-shaped stadium. A wooden fence closed in the open end of the horseshoe and at half time the crowd of knot-hole viewers outside broke the fence down. Therefore, while the record books show a paid attendance of 53,000 for the game, you can figure we had a considerably larger group on hand for the second half.

Permit me to recall just how the game progressed. My memory still is rather sharp on this game, probably because it was my best effort as a college player.

Early in the first quarter, Stanford recovered one of our fumbles on our 15-yard line. After a few line plays

31

failed, their halfback, a chap named Cuddeback, kicked a field goal and the first quarter ended Stanford 3, Notre Dame 0. However we were on the 7-yard line as the period ended, and I began the second quarter by scoring on a straight buck over center. Stanford blocked Jimmy Crowley's extra point attempt. Now it was 6-3 in our favor.

Stanford roared right back and marched deep into our territory. Ernie Nevers faded to pass and here was where Slip Madigan's scouting bore fruit. I was playing wider than I should as a linebacker. Gus Dorais, who was sitting on the bench next to Rock, commented that I was playing out of position. "He knows what he's doing," Rock told Gus. Thanks to Slip Madigan, I did. Nevers tried a screen pass. Chuck Collins, our end, deflected the ball and I caught it in mid-air. I made the catch on our 20-yard line and took off on an 80-yard sprint that made the score 12-3 before Jimmy's extra point made it 13-3. That's how it stood at half time.

Ed Hunsinger, our other end, was the hero of the third quarter. I got off a 55-yard punt to Stanford's quarterback and he dropped the ball on his own 20. Ed picked it up and raced into the end zone with Collins blocking the safety man. Again Jimmy's kick was good and our lead has stretched out to 20-3. Stanford came right back. We gambled with a pass deep in our own backyard and Stanford intercepted on our 27. Nevers ground the ball down to the three and we closed in expecting another line plunge. Ernie fooled us and passed to his end, Shipkey, for a touchdown. Cuddeback kicked the point and it was 20-10.

Stanford was on the march again as the fourth quarter opened and worked the ball down to our one-foot line. This time Nevers did plunge into the line and to this day he and a lot of other Stanford fans claim he scored. The officials ruled otherwise, but the argument still lingers on.

Many years later, a West Coast sportswriter was holding forth at a press gathering before a Notre Dame-Stanford game and insisted that Ernie Nevers was robbed.

"He was not," spoke up another man.

"How do you know?" rejoined the writer. "Just where were you sitting so you could see if he scored or not?"

"I know he didn't score because I was sitting on his head," replied the other man, who happened to be Harry Stuhldreher.

Getting the ball on our one-foot line left us only one alternative. Kick it out of there and I did, to the Stanford 48. Again the Stanford march was on with Nevers ripping apart our line, already handicapped by loss of Joe Bach with broken ribs early in the game. Once more, Ernie faded to pass and once more you know who was the receiver. I took the pass on our 30 and ran 70 yards for the final touchdown. Another of Jimmy's extra points made it 27-10 and that's how the game ended.

It was the first time in five years an Eastern school, as they considered Notre Dame, had beaten a Western school in the Rose Bowl.

We had seen Ernie Nevers for the one and only time and were mighty glad we never had to face him before or after. As for Ernie, he has this memory of the game, as quoted from a 1959 book on the Four Horsemen compiled by James A. Peterson and published by the Hinckley &

Schmitt Co. of Chicago for its annual All-Star Football Game luncheon. Said Ernie:

"The two plays that can never be erased from my memory were the two accurate passes I threw to Layden. One good for 80 yards and a touchdown and the other for 70 yards and a touchdown. A total of 150 yards in two tries and two touchdowns makes the passing combination of Layden of Notre Dame and Nevers of Stanford the best in Rose Bowl history."

Yes, that was a memorable day for Elmer Layden. All together, I had scored 18 points, which remained a Rose Bowl record until 1949 when Jack Weisenberger of Michigan tied it. After that 1949 game, a sportswriter told Weisenberger, "You know you tied Elmer Layden's record." He is supposed to have replied, "Who's Elmer Layden?"

A man of lesser modesty might have been hurt to hear that, but modesty is something all of us who played for Notre Dame in 1924 had to develop whether we wanted to or not. Our student body then was about one-fourth of the size of today's group. Football players did not live a life apart from the other students, and their achievements on the gridiron did not entitle them to any special considerations from their fellow students. This made it pretty hard to last long with a swelled head.

I remember the razzing given the first student to turn up on campus with a raccoon coat as well as the needling given the first two fellows who tried wearing knickerbocker suits. No sir, we put on a cloak of modesty. It was the only way for our egos to survive.

34

With the football season over and graduation coming up, it became of paramount concern for the Four Horsemen to begin figuring out ways to survive in the cold world once they left the university. Professional football was still in its infancy, and scouts were not descending upon the campus with fancy offers to play the pro game.

Some of you may remember that athletic stars of the 1920's often found their way into show business. Vaudeville was still in its prime, and people were willing to pay to see a famous boxer spar or shadow box as the seventh act on the bill. Inevitably, our attention was turned to the stage.

Jimmy Conzelman, who later coached the Chicago Cardinals professional team and made quite a career for himself in the advertising agency field, invited the Four Horsemen up to Chicago to audition for a vaudeville troupe that the Balaban & Katz theater chain was putting together. During Holy Week, when classes were out, the four of us went to Chicago to look into this offer.

We found that Conzelman, who was quite a piano player, had turned up sick. What kind of act he had figured out for us, we didn't learn. Maybe he thought we could do a dance routine because anybody who could master Rock's shift should have rhythm. Or maybe he wanted us to pass a football around while he played the piano. We did learn one thing: Jimmy's vaudeville act was going to play seven times a day on the B & K circuit and that sounded like a lot of work. What really ended our interest in vaudeville was the publicity picture they took of us. They brought us down to the main stage of the

Chicago Theater and had us pose as a backfield behind a line of chorus girls. The girls were not exactly overly dressed.

"If the priests at Notre Dame see this picture, we're out of school," said one of the four.

"And in Holy Week yet," said another.

We never did see the picture and sent Jimmy a get-well card informing him that we were not interested in vaudeville.

We finally did try show business, but that was in the movies, as well as pro football, which I'll touch upon later. All of us, at one time or another tried coaching.

Don Miller was an assistant coach at Georgia Tech and Ohio State before finally turning to law in his home town of Cleveland. Don loved to give speeches, and I guess he figured he could make more money talking in court than at pep talking in dressing rooms. He still gets back to Notre Dame occasionally to give a talk at a pre-game rally. Don served as the U.S. Attorney for the Northern District of Ohio at one time and now is a U.S. Referee in Bankruptcy.

Harry went East to become head coach of Villanova and, after building it into a football power, moved West again to be the top man at the University of Wisconsin for many years. His wife, Mary, wrote a book about those wild days in Madison that remains a classic account of the trials and tribulations of a coach's wife. Harry was an assistant vice-president of United States Steel Corporation when he died. Mary later was dean of women at Duquesne University and now, I'm told, is writing.

Jim Crowley, who was the wittiest of the Four Horsemen, started coaching at Georgia as an assistant, moved to head coach at Michigan State, and then to the top job at Fordham. He developed some great teams during his Fordham days including one that had a line that was nicknamed the "Seven Blocks of Granite." One of the ends on that famous line was Vince Lombardi, who went on to make quite a name for himself as coach at Green Bay, Wisconsin, which happens to be Jimmy's home town. The line coach at Fordham who also took a few bows for the "Blocks of Granite" was Frank Leahy, who later succeeded me as head coach at Notre Dame. When the All-America Conference was formed in 1945 to compete with the National Football League, Jimmy Crowley was named commissioner. By then, I was in my last year as commissioner of the NFL and two old Horsemen faced one another across the line of pro football's first big battle. This set up some interesting situations that we'll recall later. Jimmy now has left sports and is industrial development commissioner for the city of Scranton, Pennsylvania.

For myself, I was torn between coaching and law. I suspected that there came a time in every coach's career when he better have something in the way of another skill to fall back on for a living. Before resolving a career decision, of course, there was the matter of collecting my college degree. This turned out to be something of a problem.

There are several versions of why I never took the pins out of my graduation gown. Old-timers around South Bend favor this version:

My dad and I were supposed to have visited a variety of speakeasies the night before commencement. In our cups, we appropriated a horse-drawn milk wagon to get us back to the campus, whereupon I delivered a bottle of milk to every room in my residence hall. Well, this isn't true, romantic as it might sound.

What really happened was that dad went his own way the night before commencement and turned up in good shape graduation day only not to see his son Elmer in cap and gown.

Elmer had been out the night before with two of his classmates and they had visited a few places where spirits were served. On the way home to the campus, his son had filched a few—well maybe it was three or four—bottles of milk from an "abandoned" milk wagon, these bottles later to be delivered in this fashion: one was thrown against the wall of Sorin Hall, my dormitory; the other three I gave to workmen on the campus. A priest saw my first delivery and, next day, I was told I would not be graduating with my class. The day after, I talked a diploma out of the Prefect of Discipline and went back to Davenport, Iowa, with a Bachelor of Laws degree.

I had the idea of returning to Notre Dame in the fall to take some additional law courses, which I hoped to pay for with a part-time job helping coach the freshman football team.

During the summer, which I spent as a playground supervisor in Davenport, I got a call from Columbia College in Dubuque, Iowa. Eddie Anderson, an end and captain of the 1921 Notre Dame team, had been coaching Columbia and had decided to transfer to DePaul University in Chicago where he could attend Rush Medical College and become a doctor. Columbia wanted a coach, and sweetened their offer with the promise of a chance to study for the Iowa bar while working in the Dubuque law offices of Frantzen, Bonson, and Gilloon.

Just to make sure I was doing the right thing, I phoned Rock in South Bend. Looking back, I think that was kind of presumptuous on my part. Why should he care? But he did. He told me I was making a smart move.

Columbia had called the right signals. I was going to get just what I had hoped for: a crack at coaching and a chance at law.

CHAPTER FIVE

Anybody who ever coached remembers his first day on the job. My first day of coaching at Columbia College in Dubuque, Iowa was really something different. At the appointed hour for drills to begin, I walked onto the practice field to find only two players present.

"Where's the rest of the team? Or are you two the whole team?" I asked.

"The rest of the team is at choir practice," one of the boys answered.

"At choir practice!" I said.

"Sure," the boy said, "many of our boys are planning to enter the seminary, and choir practice is a required subject."

He was right. Many boys going to Columbia did enter the seminary, and several of the youngsters who played football for me in the time I was there are priests today.

Columbia then as now was operated by the Catholic Archdiocese of Dubuque. By the time I arrived it was on its fourth name, having started out as St. Raphael's College in 1839. Prior to being renamed Columbia, it had been called St. Joseph College. Wags around that part of Iowa claim the name was changed after a headline appeared on the sports page saying "Luther Trounces St. Joseph." Luther College was a member of the same conference, which was called the Western Interstate Conference.

Columbia changed its name for the fifth and final time in 1939 to Loras College and inserted an item in the by-laws that the name never could be changed again. Matthew Loras, after whom it was renamed, was the bishop of Dubuque who founded the college. For our purposes, we'll continue to call it Columbia as it was known during my two years there.

My contract called for me to coach football, basketball, and track. Baseball was the fourth sport and a priest coached it.

Home football games were played in a baseball park that was as devoid of grass as the Sahara Desert. When the weather was dry, the field was like concrete. When it rained, the field became a mudhole.

We had a rainy autumn in 1925 according to the college yearbook which reports that "one feature of the season was mud. Mud was everywhere." Even so, the yearbook hails the team as "logical claimants to the conference championship." Our conference record was three victories, one defeat, and one tie. We played three non-conference games during the season, winning one and losing two. We beat Luther in the final game for the conference title.

One game that season still sticks in my memory, the game with DePaul University in Chicago. The former Columbia coach and a former Notre Dame player, Eddie Anderson, now was coaching DePaul. We had an open date the Saturday before the DePaul game. Since I was playing in a pro game with the Brooklyn Horsemen that day, I sent my captain and quarterback, Albert Entringer, over to Chicago to scout the DePaul team. Entringer, whose nickname was "Cutie," had played for Anderson the year before. When Anderson looked over the crowd before the game, and it wasn't a very big crowd I'm told, he spotted Entringer in the stands and hollered, "Cutie, come on down and sit with me on the bench." Being the polite young man that he was, Entringer accepted the offer, and his scouting activities that day amounted to being charmed by Eddie Anderson.

DePaul beat us the next week, 12-0, on their home field, which was really something to behold in the way of a gridiron. A regulation football field is 120 yards from end zone to end zone. The goal lines are 100 yards apart and behind each is a 10-yard end zone. At that time, the goal posts were set on the goal line as they are in professional ball today. DePaul had 100 yards between the goal lines and one 10-yard end zone; the other end zone was two yards deep. It came to an abrupt halt against the solid stone wall of a building. This meant that if you scored at this short end of the field, you had to move to the other end to try for the extra point. Even though we

43

didn't score, I didn't like the looks of that tiny end zone. The defending team could practically brace themselves against the wall in a goal line stand.

We got back at DePaul the next season, beating them 8-7 on a touchdown, and a safety where we caught one of Anderson's boys behind the goal line within the confines of a regulation 10-yard end zone. Our field also had grass on it, because I had moved our home games out of that baseball park and onto our campus.

Our 1926 football season ended with four victories, two defeats and one tie. We didn't win the conference title, and Luther College beat us, 14-6, in our final game, which traditionally was played on Thanksgiving Day. Luther scored all of its points in the fourth quarter and treated me to the kind of cliff-hanger finish that years later became my trademark. What still fascinates me about the Luther squad was that nine of its first team had the last name of Olson. The Columbia yearbook, in recounting the game, commented wryly: "Perhaps Luther had one too many Olsons." It sure did.

The game I remember best is a tie. It was a scoreless tie we played with St. Thomas College in St. Paul, Minnesota. What makes it stand out in memory is that it was the first time I lost what they now would call my "cool" and took on an official. Here is what happened: Donald "Jiggs" Noonan, our quarterback threw a pass to our end, Joseph "Circus" Kellogg. The ball bounced off Kellogg, bounced off a defensive back and landed again in Kellogg's hands. The referee ruled the pass incomplete. I raced out on the field and asked the referee if my eyes were correct and the pass had hit Kellogg, hit the defense back, and then come back to Kellogg. The referee asked the umpire, who said, "Yes, that's what happened."

"What are you doing out here?" asked the referee. I told him I had raised my hand for permission. "That will be 15 yards," he said.

Instead of gaining 15 yards, we lost 30 on the play—15 we would have gained by the pass and 15 more for what the referee considered to be unsportsmanlike conduct.

There's a story about the game with St. Thomas that I like to tell. Dick Hanousek, another old teammate from the 1924 Notre Dame squad, was the St. Thomas coach. The night before the game, we had dinner together. Dick told me about the tough game they played the week before with St. Mary's College of Winona, Minnesota; how they had tried to gain ground four times with plunges through the middle of the line once they hit the other team's 20-yard line, and how each time it failed.

My parting words to my team before they left the dressing room were these: "If St. Thomas gets anywhere near our 20-yard line, look for an end run." Every time Dick's boys got near our 20, they tried an end run which we stopped, and maybe the reason the game ended in a scoreless tie is because Dick and I had dinner together the night before.

The only other time I can remember getting angry at officials was in the last college game I ever coached. That was when Notre Dame played Southern California in the Los Angeles Coliseum to close its 1940 season. We won, 10-6, before more than 85,000 people. Howard Jones was the USC coach. The athletic director was Bill Hunter and the President of the university was Dr. Rufus B. von

45

Kleinsmid. The night before the game I had been with all three of them at a pep rally because Notre Dame's relations with USC were not only of the finest, but also of long standing.

Late in the fourth quarter, USC threw a pass. Our defensive halfback broke it up. He jumped in the air with at least four USC men and, for my money, he broke it up. The field judge didn't agree. He ruled that our halfback had knocked down a receiver, that this was interference, and now it was first down on our 20-yard line with only seconds to play. We led Southern California by only four points. The Trojans had time for only a few more plays and both were incomplete passes. As the game ended, I stormed out on the field and castigated the officials as they walked to their dressing room. When Coach Howard Jones came up to me for the customary post-game congratulations, I took his hand with the warmth of an Arctic winter and said, "Howard, I've seen home town official decisions before, but never like this."

Howard could see I was boiling and made haste for the dressing room. The Layden temper, however, was not about to be cooled. At the end of the Coliseum ramp to our dressing room, I ran into President von Kleinsmid and Bill Hunter, the athletic director. Again I complained bitterly about the "homer," as we used to call home-favoring officials, that had called pass interference. Still not satisfied, I stormed in the dressing room and went to Bernie Crimmins, the back against whom the penalty was called.

Bernie, who later was an assistant coach at Notre Dame and a head coach at Indiana, could see I was burned up.

"Bernie," I said, "did you push that Southern Cal guy?"

"Yes, coach, I did," Bernie answered.

It was a thoroughly cooled Layden that ran out of his team's dressing room. First I went to the official's dressing room and apologized, then to the USC dressing room to apologize to Jones and Hunter.

"Where's President von Kleinsmid?" I asked.

"He just left for his car," Jones told me.

Fortunately, I caught him in the parking lot and managed to finish my apologies.

I never had another occasion as coach to take on an official. After that experience, I doubt that I ever would have tried.

CHAPTER SIX

Coaching at Columbia, Iowa, was teaching me that college mentors, as sportswriters were prone to call us, did not live by coaching alone. You didn't buy the good life on a coach's salary, but being a coach did open some doors to what they now call moonlighting. I was not a practicing lawyer in 1925 when I arrived in Dubuque. I was still studying for the bar examinations. This took up my mornings. Coaching took up my afternoons. A girl from Bettendorf, Iowa, was beginning to dominate my evenings. We began talking about a wedding date. Since my savings were nothing to speak of, I had the itch to put aside some extra cash.

Pro football, as I said earlier, was not then the powerful sport it is today. However, if ever the historians of pro football pick any year prior to the end of World War II when the game had a spurt of success, it has to be 1925.

That was the year Red Grange finished up at Illinois and went from college football one day to pro football the next. Red joined the Chicago Bears and the record books show that the Bears toured Red around the country for a grand total of fourteen post-season games.

The same record book lists fifteen professional teams that were active during the 1925 season as well as five others that may or may not have played, but didn't send in the scores. In my case, the most notable pro team of the year was the Rock Island Independents, located across the Mississippi River from my home town and not far down the river from Dubuque. Rock Island had booked a game with Wilson's Wildcats, a team of West Coast college stars led by Wildcat Wilson, who had been a standout player at the University of Washington. I was approached as to my availability to play for the Independents and ended up signing a contract for $1,500 to play in this one, single game. Grange hadn't graduated from Illinois yet, so this set an early pay record for a single professional appearance. The sum of $1,500 for a single game was of such magnitude that the Rock Island club even hired a photographer to get a picture of me signing.

The Independents had a pretty fine ball club. Duke Slater, one of the first Negro All-Americans and an alltime star at Iowa, played one tackle. A giant of a man from Washington and Jefferson, named Weiderquist, played the other. Lou Kolls, a well-known sandlot player from the Quad Cities area as well as a major league baseball umpire, was the center.

Lou was the last center I can remember who passed

the ball back in end-over-end fashion. On defense that day, my position was linebacker. Behind the line Rock Island had, this amounted to a pleasant afternoon in a rocking chair. I didn't have to budge. Nobody got past the bunch in front of me. We won, 7-3. My only accomplishment was having a punt blocked after I fumbled one of Kolls' dipsy-doodle passes from center, and this shook my ego somewhat. I always considered myself an excellent punter, and during three years of college competition never had a punt blocked.

A taste of moonlight money only whetted my appetite for more. Harry Stuhldreher also was picking up extra cash in pro games and talked me into coming East to play with an All Star team made up of former Notre Dame players. Our opponent was Pottsville, Pennsylvania, which claimed the professional championship that year. The game ended in disaster for everybody concerned. The league stripped Pottsville of its title for playing an unauthorized post-season game and the promoter wandered off with the gate receipts without stopping by to pay off the participants. Undaunted, many of us were in uniform the next day playing for the Hartford (Conn.) Blues against the Cleveland Indians in Hartford. Two pro games in two consecutive days sounds like a lot of football and it was.

During my two seasons coaching at Columbia, I made myself available for a little extracurricular football whenever the schedule permitted. I was not alone. Many coaches did it. I've heard it said that during one pro season, Rock played for a different team on six different Sundays. Even some college players were known to appear on Sunday afternoons in different uniforms and under assumed names.

My last appearance of major consequence as a pro was on New Year's Day, 1926, when a group of former Notre Dame players were matched against a team of former Princeton players at Coral Gables, Florida. I got $1,500 for that game, too, largely because I was the last one to sign up. The earlier toilers in the vineyard were paid much less. We had to show up a week or so ahead of the game to practice, which again was rather unusual for professional teams of that era. As a result of these practice sessions, I had to miss the start of basketball practice at Columbia and my team there showed it. We lost our first seven games.

One of the candidates for basketball that season was Don Ameche. Don did not make the varsity, but he did carve out quite a career for himself in the movies. A long time friend of Arch Ward, Don was one of the first people to bankroll a team in the All-America Conference, when the rival pro league started up in 1945. His team was the Los Angeles Dons and, unfortunately for Don, they did not survive the merger with the National Football League that came five years later. Columbia's basketball record during both years I coached was nine victories and six defeats.

During the summer of 1926, I passed the Iowa bar examinations. In October that year, I also married Edythe Davis of Bettendorf in the Columbia College chapel. It was a big enough occasion to have the college declare a free day from classes. The student body presented me with a wedding gift: a black German shepherd dog. This was the first of a series of dogs that plagued my life. I spent more on rewards for their return than I did on dog food.

As the spring of 1927 came around, a little Layden was on the way, and I was beginning to investigate a better coaching job. Such a job was materializing in, of all places, New Castle, Pennsylvania. Father Martin Brennan, an assistant pastor in a Catholic church there, had set himself up as an unofficial scout to find a new coach for his alma mater, Duquesne University. Father Brennan brought the subject up to one of his parishioners, Joe Green, who had been my roommate one year at Notre Dame. Joe threw my name into the hat and before long, I was contacted by Duquesne.

On August 20, 1927, I signed a two-year contract to be athletic director and head football coach at Duquesne for the then-munificent sum of $6,500 a year. Reading over the terms of that contract, I notice that I was not to participate in professional football nor devote more than three hours a day to football practice between August and December. I thought of my law background as a way of earning extra funds, until I checked and found I would have to pass the Pennsylvania bar exams to practice in that state. I never did try and my legal sideline came to a quiet close as wife, baby daughter and coach packed the family car for the trip to Pittsburgh, a journey that eventually would lead back to Notre Dame.

CHAPTER SEVEN

Duquesne University, founded in 1879 by the Holy Ghost Fathers, sits high on a bluff near the downtown area of Pittsburgh. The name is properly pronounced "Due-Kane," though many an early radio sportscaster was known to call it "Due-Kwess-Knee." In 1927, it rated a distant third in the interests of Pittsburgh sports fans, well behind the University of Pittsburgh and the Carnegie Institute of Technology.

Varsity football had languished to a point where the team had only eleven jerseys with numbers and only enough other spare parts to make up 35 makeshift uniforms. The athletic field had been built over an old brick yard and resembled a junk yard more than a gridiron. Part of it was naked of grass; the remainder was covered with a form of tumbleweed. My first day on the scene I was cautioned by a student manager about kicking extra points. When the ball cleared the goal posts at one end of the field, it plunged 500 feet or so down the bluff. You had to have a streak of mountain goat in you to be a football manager at that university.

A situation that at first glance looked pretty bleak soon turned out to have some bright spots. First there was the president, Father Martin Hehir (pronounced Hair), who had promised his full cooperation and did all he could to keep that promise. Then there was Hugh Muldoon, dean of the college of pharmacy, which ranked with the best in the nation, a real lover of football who wanted to see Duquesne rise to prominence. Added to this pair of backers were two men of lesser rank in the university's scheme of things, but mighty helpful in getting things done: Brother Ammon and "Brue" Jackson.

Brother Ammon was a humble man who had chosen the route of a brother rather than that of a priest to fulfill his vocation in religious life. His vocation in the university's life was being helpful to its athletic teams. When we tried to improve the athletic field and enlarge the seating, Brother Ammon took on the job. When we played a home game, my wife parked the baby and her bottle with Brother Ammon, who gave up the chance to see his team play to be the coach's babysitter.

Cleveland Kim "Brue" Jackson is a story by himself. Brue was the first Negro to become the starting quarterback at Braddock High School just outside of Pittsburgh. Brue's dad wanted him to go to college, and so Brue dutifully presented himself at Duquesne in 1925 because it was then what now is called integrated. How it came to be integrated, nobody seems to remember. Brue says he

The picture that made us Four Horsemen, taken by request of George Strickler the Monday after we beat Army in 1924, and Granny Rice (at George's suggestion) had given us a nickname that's lasted ever since. Left to right: Miller, Layden, Crowley and Stuhldreher.

About the last time the Horsemen got together was at the dedication of the Professional Football Hall of Fame in Canton, Ohio. Left to right: Layden, Miller, Stuhldreher and Crowley.

The Indian is Jim Thorpe, the greatest football player of them all, who was in Hollywood at the same time in 1931 making an epic called "Battling with Buffalo Bill." The others left to right are me, Adam Walsh, Captain of the 1924 team, Frank Carideo, of the 1930 Notre Dame team, Harry, Don and Jimmy.

The "immortal" Will Rogers had us as guests at his ranch during our stay in Hollywood. Here, Will tries roping Jimmy, who has the ball. The others, from left, Don, me, Harry and Adam.

This was taken at the 1925 Rose Bowl game. The guy with the ball looks like Harry sneaking out-of-bounds to get a better field position. The official at left is wearing plaid knickers.

61

The day I signed with the Rock Island Independents for $1,500 for a single game. The man behind me is my dad, Tom Layden, who probably was ready to rush the check to the bank to make sure it was good. At left is Walter Archer, secretary of the Rock Island Chamber of Commerce. The fellow on the right is A. H. Bowlby, managing secretary of the team.

thinks it may be because the Holy Ghost Fathers also ran missions in Africa. Whatever the reason, Brue was not the first Negro to apply for admission. Others were already there, and three Negroes were on the football squad when I arrived as coach. Three of my better linemen on the 1929 team—Sammy Pratt, Moko Lesser, and Leo Silverstein—would not show up for the West Virginia game because it fell on Yom Kippur. The priests who ran Duquesne were not in the business of letting color or creed get in the way of education.

Brue Jackson wanted to be a doctor and hoped to get a pre-medical education. After looking around at his chances for an athletic scholarship, Brue made himself a different deal: he would be the athletic trainer in return for an education. Unfortunately, many of the laboratory classes that were required in the pre-med course fell during the afternoon period when Brue was tied up in his trainer duties. He never did get a degree of any kind from the university, but he remained a fixture of the athletic department there until Duquesne gave up varsity football in 1951.

Notre Dame had an active alumni group in Pittsburgh and through these people I came across another fine booster, Dr. Leo O'Donnell, a Notre Dame graduate who was a top surgeon at Mercy Hospital near the Bluff, as they called the Duquesne campus. During the next seven years, Dr. O'Donnell, Brue and I did some serious experimenting in the care and protection of football players.

Frank P. McDermott, a student in the law school, had coached varsity football until I arrived and he left me with some good talent. Foremost was the center of the

1926 team, a fellow named Aldo "Buff" Donnelli. Buff was reputed to be one of the finest amateur soccer players in the United States. When the British brought a soccer team to Pittsburgh to play an amateur team, Buff was in the starting lineup for the local team. He could kick and, at this point, I must confess that I have always had a soft spot in my heart for kickers. I liked to kick and during my college days did a good deal of the punting for Notre Dame. Afterwards, a good kicker drew me to his attention like a magnet. Donnelli liked to kick soccer style, moving into the ball from a side angle. Had he come along thirty years or so later, he would have been the darling of football, as soccer-style kickers have been during the 1960's. At the time, I switched his style to make him kick square into the ball, and he became a fine kicker for Duquesne. I also switched him from center to fullback because the boy was a good runner and it was obviously not possible to center the ball, run back to catch it and then run or kick it. Switching Donnelli from center to fullback was my smartest move in 1927. He benefited and so did I. They still remember him fondly on the Bluff because Buff later coached Duquesne as well as the Pittsburgh Steelers professional team.

One of the toughest jobs I had to perform as Commissioner of the National Football League was asking Buff to make up his mind about which team he was going to coach. At the time, and this was during World War II, he was coaching the Steelers for pay and Duquesne for free. Buff chose his old college when the chips were down. He later coached Boston University and spent years as successor to Lou Little as head coach of Columbia University in New York City until he resigned recently.

For the first time, I was not coaching alone. When Duquesne let me hire an assistant I asked Johnny Weibel to come up from Vanderbilt University in Nashville, Tennessee. Johnny had been a guard on our 1924 Notre Dame team. He was studying medicine at Vanderbilt, and was an assistant under that fine coach Dan McGuigan. He was looking for some action and he readily moved to Pittsburgh, where he was invaluable both as a line coach and as a scout. He spent the first year with me, then returned to Vanderbilt to get his M.D. degree, immediately to return to Pittsburgh to intern at Mercy Hospital under Doc O'Donnell. Johnny hovered on the scene while my first son, Elmer Jr., was born and then died tragically of a ruptured appendix before finishing his internship. Bob Reagan succeeded Johnny, and Joe Bach later replaced Bob who left us to become a head coach himself.

I won't bore you with a game-by-game replay of our 1927 football schedule. It opened with a loss to St. Bonaventure in Olean, N.Y. and ended with a defeat by Ashland College. The season record: four victories, four defeats, one tie.

The 1928 season was a different story. By now, I had learned that you have to do a little recruiting to be a successful coach. By now, I had also managed to squeeze thirty-six football scholarships out of the treasurer of Duquesne, Father J. P. Danner, who was fondly known then as "Old Tight-Fist" Danner, who practiced the vow of poverty he had taken to enter the Holy Ghost Fathers.

We had about thirty-five or forty candidates for football at the start of the 1927 season. We had more than 250 candidates for the start of the 1928 season. Word had spread through the hills of Pennsylvania that a disciple of Knute Rockne had arrived at Duquesne, bent on making a football power. For the first and only time as a coach, I staged tryouts. I had only thirty-six scholarships to give and I explained first that we did not have an engineering school. This made no impact since most of my candidates had come to me after visiting other tryout camps run by Pitt and Carnegie Tech.

The package I could offer these boys consisted of tuition and room and board in return for playing football and working at a part-time job. Their room really was a cot in the gymnasium until basketball season began. After that, they were relegated to a loft above the main building; or, if they were especially lucky, Dean Muldoon might put them up in his apartment. Many of these youngsters came from the coal fields of Pennsylvania. They had no desire to follow their dads into the mines. They left home with the clothes on their backs and little else. They were not expected to return, and Duquesne was their last stop in search of three square meals and an opportunity to keep away from the mines.

Not only did I have talent rolling in, I also managed to book a big-time game for my team. With the help of "Fats" Henry, the athletic director, and Andy Kerr, the coach, I was able to plug an open date with Washington and Jefferson.

W and J was still a football power in the East. Our 1928 game was billed by Harry Keck, sports editor of the Pittsburgh *Sun-Telegraph*, this way: "After years of trying, Duquesne University finally has broken the ice and landed a football game with one of the major elevens of the district. This is a good break for the Dukes. It is the forerunner of bigger and better things. It may lead eventually to annual meetings with Pitt and Carnegie Tech."

At last, Duquesne was going to play one of the big teams.

CHAPTER EIGHT

They don't play football anymore the way it was played at Washington and Jefferson in October, 1928. There may have been some seats along the field, but nobody used them. The spectators followed the teams up and down the field. "They were practically selling popcorn in our back-field," is the way I described it afterwards. Shortly after the kickoff, I tried to find a seat on our bench. It was occupied by a striking blonde in a leopard skin coat. I called over a student manager and said, "Get rid of the gal in the leopard skin coat." She took care of the manager with a flutter of eyelashes, and I had to get a substitute for him to move her off the bench.

We really got the team up for this game. Brue Jackson tells me the team broke down the dressing room door after my pep talk. I can't remember that this really happened. The dressing room was a shed at one end of the field, and even if my oratory did arouse the team, it wouldn't have taken much to knock down the door.

All week long we had practiced pass plays, and my favorite pass-catching end, Joe Greer, was suffering from fumblelitis. "Concentrate, Joe," I'd holler at him. The more he concentrated, the more he dropped passes.

I had cooked up a trick play for our bunch and this one time it worked. We won the toss and chose to receive. Doggo Burns was put on the sideline without a head gear. He was told to stay near the head linesman and be inconspicuous. The way the crowd milled up and down the sidelines, this instruction was unnecessary. After returning the kickoff, our team went right into formation and the quarterback, Ganzy Benedict, threw a long pass to Burns, whom nobody had noticed missing as we had lined up. He caught it and we were inside the W and J 20-yard line. A few plays later, we scored. Little old Duquesne was leading mighty Washington and Jefferson, 6-0, on the old hidden player trick.

W and J did not die that easily. Before we knew it, they had scored, too, kicked the extra point, and led us, 7-6. Most of the remainder of the game was grind, grunt, and punt. The home team still led us late in the fourth quarter. The crowd meanwhile was all over the field. The end zone was filled with spectators as we made a last desperate effort to score. Benedict called a pass to Greer. He faded back and let loose with a toss into that crowded end zone. Who should jump out of the crowd to take it but Greer. "How was that for concentration, coach!" yelled Ray Kemp, one of our tackles, as he pounded me on the back. Final score: Duquesne 12, Washington and Jefferson

7; a real upset and the start of something big on the Bluff. Before long, we had Pitt on the schedule. Carnegie Tech never did sign up in my time, but we did play them in a 1931 post-season game for charity. It was a scoreless tie. Pitt beat us both times we played while I was coaching Duquesne.

For the record, we opened the 1928 season with Slippery Rock. Yes, there was and still is a Slippery Rock State Teachers College.

Our season record was eight victories and one defeat . . . by Geneva coached then by Alvin "Bo" McMillen, who later gained greater fame at Indiana and the Detroit Lions. Bo's Geneva team the next year helped us introduce night football into Pittsburgh.

Once you get a taste of the big time, you begin to wonder how you can make it pay off. Father Danner, our treasurer, was beginning to wonder when this team that had beaten Washington and Jefferson was going to begin returning some revenue. So was I. Both of us knew it was nearly impossible to expect a big box office return from games we played on our home field. At best, 5,000 people could fit in. The time had come to see just what kind of attraction Duquesne football really was in the Pittsburgh area.

John D. Holahan, my student manager of athletics in 1927, had stayed as graduate manager of athletics. I've been told that John borrowed money from his dad to help us rent Forbes Field for our first night game. Forbes Field, then as now, was the home of the Pittsburgh Pirates baseball team. As such, it had some grass, which put it way ahead of our home field. We scheduled the 1929 Geneva game for a Friday night at Forbes Field. Riding a wave of optimism, we printed 10,000 tickets, twice as many as we had been selling. We ran out of tickets long before the kickoff. Our attendance for this first experiment in football under lights was later placed at 27,000.

Geneva gave everybody a thrill when their star halfback, a chap named Knappick, ran the opening kickoff 97 yards back for a touchdown. That was the only time they scored. We won, 27-7. And thereafter, Duquesne played all of its home games at Forbes Field, usually under lights. Our team's nickname changed from the "Dukes" to the "Night Riders." To capitalize on this new name, I had the team's picture taken on horses. Instead of four men on horses, we took a picture of eleven men on horses. George Strickler's idea of five years earlier was good enough to imitate. Since Father Danner did not have funds for the rental of horses, we borrowed them from the mounted unit of the Pittsburgh Police Department. You could see the billy clubs hanging from the saddle cloths.

Besides night football, we also experimented with other innovations. Doc O'Donnell was the team physician and, together with Brue Jackson, we tried various concoctions to serve the team at half time to revitalize their energy. The doctor favored glucose, but it was so sickly sweet that we soon gave it up. Brue, who by this time had become sort of a curbstone physician, favored honey, because, as he said, it was pre-digested by the bees and hit the bloodstream immediately. Finally, we settled on fresh oranges as the best warm weather pick-me-up. During cold weather, Brue served hot bouillon. Not until 1968 did I learn that he and Doc O'Donnell spiked it with a half-

gallon of wine. "On those cold days, we sure had a spir-
ited team in the second half," Brue says. Now that he has
confessed, I guess we did.

Our experiments in what might be called the paramedi-
cal side of football were not limited to half-time pick-
me-ups. We probably had one of the first college football
teams that was fed salt tablets on hot days, an idea that
came to us via Doc O'Donnell right out of the steel mills
around Pittsburgh where men working in intense heat
took them.

We tried a variety of ways to prevent football injuries.
These included exercises aimed at limbering up and
toughening up our players' necks and knees and ankles.
We experimented with a solution devised to prevent irri-
tation of the skin on areas where we applied tape to the
legs, shoulders, and ankles.

One summer we managed to talk Father Danner out of
enough money to send Brue Jackson to the New York
Polyclinic Hospital for a two-week seminar for athletic
trainers. Brue reported later that his daily diet during the
course consisted of a box of ginger snaps and a bottle of
milk because our stipend was not large enough to take
care of meals.

My wildest experiment at Duquesne was trying soccer
pants on my backfield. Soccer pants then looked like long
Bermuda shorts. I had the idea they gave more freedom
of movement for runners than conventional football
pants. We taped knee pads and thigh pads to our boys
and then had them wear these short, loose-fitting pants.
They not only looked funny, they also didn't result in any
faster running, so we abandoned them after a brief test.

But one thing we did do at Duquesne was try, not only to win football games, but also to make the game safer for our players. I'd like to think we were way ahead of our time in the latter respect.

CHAPTER NINE

One day I'll never forget is March 31, 1931. Around noon, Regis Welsh, sports editor of the Pittsburgh *Post-Gazette,* called me up and said, "Rock was just killed in a plane crash."

"Are you sure?" I asked.

"Well, hang on and I'll check it again," Welsh replied.

He came back within a minute and confirmed the fact that Knute Rockne indeed had died in an airline crash in Kansas.

All of the nation was stunned, for Rock had become a national figure. He had risen above his role as a football coach to become a symbol of sportsmanship and fair play to millions around the country. Joe Bach, a tackle on the 1924 team who had become my assistant at Duquesne, walked into my office and we locked the door and personally mourned a man who had come to be more than just a coach to us. Rock never came to Pittsburgh without stopping by or at least calling up. When he was going to give a speech in town, we managed to take some of our team to hear it. When Notre Dame opened its new stadium in 1930, my Duquesne team had favored seats at the dedicatory game. We had played Loyola of Chicago the night before in Chicago, but the high point of the trip for us was seeing Notre Dame beat Navy in the game that formally opened the new stadium.

The passage of time dims the memory of a lot of us, and I'm still asked if Rock didn't get killed in a plane crash with Wiley Post.

"No, that was Will Rogers," I have to reply. Will was a great friend of Rock's and later became a friend of mine.

When retirement caught up with me in the spring of 1968 and I began cleaning out my office, I ran into several books written both by Rock and about him. In one I found a few yellowed typewritten sheets of paper setting up hypothetical situations for quarterbacks, such as: The ball is on your 35-yard line; it is third down with three yards to go; what will you do? This is what Rock used to do with his quarterbacks, a tactic I borrowed later in every coaching job I had; set up situations and see what the quarterback will do. This was a forerunner of what today is called the "two-minute drill" whereby quarterbacks are expected to outline a series of plays and strategies to score within the last two minutes of the game. In Rock's time and in my coaching days, quarterbacks really called most of the plays. There was no free substitution rule in which each play could be sent in from the bench. In fact, for many years, a substitute entering the game was not permitted to speak in the huddle for at least one play after he had entered. Coaching from the bench was a foul.

I bring up Rock's quarterback quiz only because many old-timers have heard a famous story about it. The story goes like this: During one of these skull sessions, Rock is supposed to have turned to the sixth team quarterback, who looked like he was day dreaming, and asked him: "What would you do in this situation?"

The quarterback is supposed to have answered: "I'd rub some more resin into my pants so I wouldn't fall off the bench."

Well, I remember hearing almost exactly that same line, but it wasn't from a quarterback, but from Rex Enright, one of the fullbacks on our team at Notre Dame. One rainy day before we went out on the field, we saw Enright dusting his pants with resin and somebody asked why. "So I won't slide off that wet bench," he answered.

The Four Horsemen managed to get back to South Bend for Rock's funeral. Each of us felt a personal loss because Rock had continued to help us with ideas and suggestions and advice in the years we had been gone from Notre Dame. Certainly, each of us would do anything we could for him. Now that he was gone, we felt the same way about his widow, Bonnie, and his family.

Then came the odd way we were asked to help out. On the fringe of Notre Dame there always existed a group of promoters, looking for some way to cash in on the school's fame or the success of its players or coaches. Fortunately for the university, these promoters generally used fairly good taste, or the people they were trying to promote insisted upon them using good taste. One such promoter was Christy Walsh, a California alumnus who hovered in the Rockne background for some years serving, among other things, as a ghost writer. Christy got the idea that a movie should be made about Rock.

I'm told that one of the reasons for the air trip Rock took that ended in his death was discussion with one of the big movie companies about playing the role of a coach in a movie version of the play, "Good News." When the play had been on Broadway, Rock had stepped into the cast one night to give the coach's pep talk, which was one of the highlights of this show.

By the summer of 1931, following Rock's death in March, Christy Walsh had become the promoter and casting director of a film that was titled "The Spirit of Notre Dame" and produced by Universal studios. This was the first of two movies about Rock, and all critical opinion seems to agree it was the poorer of the two. About all you can say about it is that it did have the original cast. The only person missing was Rock. Before Christy was done, he had lined up Mrs. Rockne and the 1924 team including the Four Horsemen. Once again, I was the last to sign.

The film was shot during the summer of 1931, which was not my idea of the season of the year to visit California. The salary offer Christy gave me as well as the others also was not my idea of a movie star's salary. During these early Depression years, it seemed that movie stars were the only people making any kind of money in this country, and so you would think anybody would jump at the idea of being in pictures. I was set to jump until I heard the pay: $7.50 a day, which I learned from a man in the movie business in Pittsburgh to be the going rate for "extras" in Hollywood. No sir, I wasn't signing.

I took the family back to Davenport to spend our summer vacation only to be barraged by letters, wires, and phone calls begging me to join the other Horsemen and come to Hollywood. When it reached the point where the wives were being invited, too, the pressure built up at home. At last, I relented and we boarded a Pullman car for movieland with the others. Let me tell you this was one hot train ride. Air conditioning had not yet arrived, and the trip across the California desert in mid-summer still is baked in my memory. What burned me up first was Christy's demand that we take upper and lower berths. This movie star was not about to ride West in that fashion. Finally, Christy coughed up some compartments. The day we passed through Yuma, Arizona, the temperature was 120 degrees. We were gasping for air out of the windows and getting a face full of hot cinders for our trouble. I happened to check Christy's drawing room to find Mrs. Walsh being cooled by a fan blowing over a cake of ice. The promoter's wife was riding in style. The Four Horsemen were being roasted.

We finally did make a movie that not only did not win an Oscar, it didn't even come close. J. Farrell McDonald, a veteran character actor, played the part of Rock. He bore a striking resemblance to him, too. Pat O'Brien, who played the part nine years later in the second Rockne movie, had to resort to heavy makeup to turn his Irish face into a reasonable facsimile of Rock's looks. Pat, however, managed to do a remarkable impersonation of Rock's speech, an impersonation that was so good he uses it to this day to charm audiences. One of the big roles in both films was the part of George Gipp. Ronald Reagan played it in the second version, which was titled "Knute Rockne, All American." He since has gone on to bigger and better things as governor of California. I can bet anybody they can't remember who played the part of Gipp in the first film. Of course, it's an unfair bet since so many people alive today have been deprived of seeing this epic. It hasn't even made the late-late show. Well, the answer is Lew Ayres, who was riding the crest of his performance in "All Quiet on the Western Front" and probably never has mentioned his role in the first Rockne film, even to his closest friends.

The Four Horsemen were played by the real guys. Adam Walsh, who played center and was captain of the 1924 team, was the only genuine member of the Seven Mules who performed. The rest of the cast was drawn from Southern California football players and actors who had appeared in "All Quiet on the Western Front," turning this latter bunch from Huns in one movie to Fighting Irish in the other.

The Hollywood experience did have a few pleasant moments. First we were introduced to the tricks a camera can be made to play. We were lined up to kick the point after a touchdown. One of us asked, "What happens if the ball doesn't go through the goal posts like it should?"

"Just kick it," the director said, "we'll make it go through the goal posts."

The real highlight of this expedition was a visit to Will Rogers' ranch. The old cowboy had a stableful of polo ponies, and the movie's press agent insisted that the Four Horsemen ride again. I begged for and got the quietest animal of the bunch because, confidentially, I've never been too brave riding horses. Next to flying, about which I remain a devout coward, I like riding a horse least. Yet it always seemed that whenever Stuhldreher, Crowley, Miller, and Layden got together, someone wanted to put us on horses.

A few years ago, I served for a time as a director of a night harness horse track. I had barely attended my first board meeting before Ed Walsh, the track's publicity director, asked me to ride again. This time I was lucky. I got to ride in a sulky behind the horse rather than on the horse's back.

On the twenty-fifth anniversary of the Four Horsemen, we arrived at the Notre Dame campus on a bitterly cold afternoon with eight inches of snow on the ground, only to be met by four horses and an anxious photographer who immediately mounted us on them.

Our visit to Will Rogers' place, after the horses and picture-taking was out of the way, was thoroughly delightful. Out of it grew a friendship with Will that lasted through the few years he had left on this earth. He very kindly came to speak at the Notre Dame football banquet the first year I coached there and was his brilliant, comic self. Yet he reached the high point that evening when he eulogized Rock, whom he had first met in 1922 when he was starring in the Ziegfeld Follies and Rock had been brought backstage to visit the cast. Our whole squad attended the show as guests of Joseph M. Byrne, a Notre Dame alumnus who served as a sort of guardian to us when we were in New York. Will noted our presence by doing his lasso twirling act wearing a Notre Dame monogrammed sweater.

Once the movie was over, our tinsel world returned to normal and after another hot Pullman trip we were home again, thoroughly surprised by the fact that Christy Walsh had a last minute pang of charity and gave us each a $200 bonus for our acting.

I can claim another distinction at this point. I also appeared in the second Rockne movie, circa 1940, this time playing the part of the coach of Notre Dame, which I was at the time. The team and I came on during the last ten or twenty seconds of the film. I was shown getting up off my knees from the pre-game huddle presumably after we had said our usual pre-game prayer. I put on a felt fedora that by today's standards has a brim wide enough to be on a ten-gallon hat. Unlike today's coaches, we got dressed up for a game. Coaches today sort of pride themselves on looking sloppy. They wear all kinds of sweat shirts, old pants, and baseball caps whereas in my time, we dressed up. I remember one season at Duquesne when I wore a black Chesterfield overcoat, white silk scarf and black derby hat on the cold days. Never can I recall coaching a game without a necktie. Brue Jackson tells me that I set such an example that he wore a fresh white shirt and black bow tie himself, which probably made him one of the best dressed trainers of the era.

I still get what you might call a "residual" from this second film role. At least once a year, somebody calls me during the middle of the night to tell me they've just seen me on the late-late show.

CHAPTER TEN

When I was coaching college football, the place to coach was Notre Dame. Every alumnus dreamed of the day he would be tapped for the job. Even today, the job is still sought after. I'm told Ara Parseghian actively pursued it, and certainly his record shows that he was magnificently qualified. When Terry Brennan abruptly was dismissed, there were several rumors that he was considering another coaching job. John P. Carmichael, sports editor of the *Chicago Daily News,* quashed them all in his column by stating, "This would be like President Eisenhower running for the House of Representatives." For a college coach, Notre Dame is the zenith, or it certainly was in 1933 when I was hired.

There are several versions of how I came to be the choice. The most repeated runs like this:

A distinguished group of a half dozen influential alumni

was asked to submit a list of candidates. While my name did not appear first on any of these lists, it did appear somewhere on every list. Thus I became the consensus choice. This story may or may not be true. I never bothered to check. Here is how I remember it:

Duquesne's regular season had ended for 1933 and while we had two post-season games ahead, I was able to get down to New York for the Army-Notre Dame game. Shortly after I checked into the Commodore hotel, Father John O'Hara called me and asked me to join him for dinner. Father O'Hara was vice president of the university and, as such, in charge of the athletic board. Because Father Charles O'Donnell then was seriously ill, O'Hara also was serving as acting president. Father O'Hara was what you had to call quite a guy, as well as quite a priest. First of all, he was a humble man whose big ambition always was to be a parish priest. Since he belonged to the Holy Cross Fathers, the order that runs Notre Dame, he had but a slight chance to fulfill this ambition because the Holy Cross Fathers operate few parish churches. Yet Father O'Hara was not to be prevented from what he liked to do best—he turned the university into his parish. He became what was called Prefect of Religion and served as pastor to the student body. He made himself available at all hours to hear confession and serve as a counselor to a student in need of either spiritual or temporal advice. He began the Notre Dame Religious Bulletin, which he wrote in such a peppy style that it was widely quoted elsewhere and became a fixture of Notre Dame student life. Whatever hopes he might have had of getting a parish to run were ended in 1940 when he was named Auxiliary Bishop of New York to serve as Cardinal Spellman's assistant in overseeing U.S. military chaplains. After the war, he was made bishop of Buffalo, then archbishop of Philadelphia and finally a cardinal, the first member of his religious order ever to get the red hat. With all of these greater responsibilities and higher honors, he never forgot Notre Dame, and today is buried in a crypt near the main altar of Sacred Heart Church on the campus.

Father O'Hara put it to me straight off at dinner that night. Would I consider becoming head football coach and athletic director at Notre Dame? You can imagine the answer that jumped in my throat. Yet I could not say, "yes," until I found out more about the situation. The head coach was Heartley W. "Hunk" Anderson, an old friend. The athletic director was Jesse Harper, who had been called off his Kansas ranch to fill part of the void left by Rock's death. Suddenly I felt like I might be sneaking behind the backs of my friends. I never considered myself to be that kind of guy, and I wasn't about to start.

Hunk Anderson had had a dismal season in 1933, winning only two games and tying one, while losing five. This was his last game and, I might add, he upset Army, 13-12, before a capacity crowd at Yankee Stadium. Even so, Father O'Hara told me, the university administration had decided that it was going to make a change. Hunk knew it and Jesse Harper knew it, he said. Now it was up to me. Did I want the job or didn't I? Satisfied it would be me or somebody else, I agreed to meet Father O'Hara a few weeks later at his mother's house in Indianapolis to sign the contract.

Duquesne still had two post-season games ahead of it.

The first was a charity game in St. Louis against a team of Purdue all-stars. The train passed through Indianapolis on the way West, and I dropped off to see Father O'Hara where we signed the contract on a table he told me was more than 100 years old that his mother had brought from Ireland. Next to signing over the Blarney Stone, this must have been about as appropriate a place as you could find to sign up a coach for the Fighting Irish.

The news of my new job hit the Pittsburgh newspapers with quite a splash. When I had arrived, I was lucky to be talked about on the sports pages. When I left, it was front page news. One newspaper even took the effort to come out to our house and interview my daughter, Joan, who then was six years old. Here are some excerpts from that interview:

"Did you know that your daddy is going to Notre Dame to coach the football team?"

"He is not," said Joan. "I know he isn't because he didn't tell me about it."

At that point, two little boys who were listening to this conversation volunteered that Pitt was the best football team around.

"My daddy has a better football team," said Joan.

When pressed further by the reporter, Joan admitted she knew somebody at Notre Dame. "My Uncle Mike plays football at Notre Dame and he's going to give my brother a real football with his name on it."

Her brother, Elmer Jr., then age three, was asleep at the time and had no comment. The reporter pressed on and asked Joan if she minded leaving Pittsburgh. Looking at her two playmates who earlier had boomed the Pitt team, she is quoted as replying: "I think I'll be glad to go to get away from these boys."

We won the charity game, which was run for a boys' club by a Monsignor Wagner down in St. Louis, and then began workouts for the first bowl game to which Duquesne ever had been invited. They then called it the Festival of Palms; today they call it the Orange Bowl. We went into the game with a record of nine victories and one defeat, the latter administered by good old Pitt, which had been on our schedule for two seasons now and won both games. Our bowl opponent was the University of Miami, and, after an even first half, we had no trouble disposing of them, 33 to 7.

Bob Zuppke of Illinois served as an assistant coach to Miami for this game and spent most of the first half yelling at the officials, "Watch that shift!" Zupp was not to be converted to anybody's shift—Rock's or mine.

This was my last bowl game, but not the last one for Duquesne. They were back at the Orange Bowl in 1936, a year that saw Pitt go to the Rose Bowl and Carnegie Tech to the Sugar Bowl; the only time three college teams from the same city ever received bowl invitations.

Before we leave the Bluff, I should say a word about track, which I also coached. With Brother Ammon's help, we laid out a 330-yard track around our football field. The standard track is 440 yards, but the confines of our old brick yard did not permit this.

Even so, we had some interesting track teams, the most interesting being my so-called two-man track team of Joe Pesci and Tom Schnellbach. Pesci could run the half mile, the mile and the two mile in a single afternoon and do well in all of them. Schnellbach ran every sprint up to the quarter mile, and with both of them we could pile up a respectable point total.

Besides introducing track to the athletic program, I started a golf team. I also started a Monogram Club, similar to the one at Notre Dame, made up of students who had won their letter in one or the other sports. Notre Dame's Monogram Club has been a great source of continued fellowship and association among its athletes after they are graduated. Even though football is gone from the Bluff, I'm told there still is a Monogram Club, and I hope it continues to thrive. We also started a Catholic high school basketball league in Pittsburgh and conducted the first state-wide tournament. The winner was sent to the national Catholic high school tournament in Chicago.

When I coached at Duquesne, they called me the "Zipper." Now that forty years have gone by, I can't for the life of me remember how I got that nickname. Later on, I was called the "Thin Man of Notre Dame." I'd like to think I can still qualify for that title even though I may weigh a few pounds more now than I did then.

The whole Duquesne student body turned out at the gymnasium to send me off to Notre Dame. My departure even was broadcast over a local radio station. The president of the university spoke. His vice-president spoke. Joe Bach, who had been named to succeed me, spoke. The head cheerleader led cheers. Yet what really choked me up was Brue Jackson, who sang a song. Brue had often entertained our team with his songs and piano playing. Already he was picking up a side dollar doing night club work and later made quite a name for himself in show business. This particular day, he was on at the end of the program and sang, "I Wish I Had My Old Pal Back Again."

Certainly I was leaving a lot of old pals, and I never did meet a better bunch than the Dean Muldoons, the Doc O'Donnells, and the Brue Jacksons, nor the boys on the team I was leaving behind.

Let me confess that I had a sneaky desire to steal one of these boys when I left. His name is Mike Basrak, and he later became the first football player at Duquesne to be named an All-American. Mike was a center and came to us, as many boys did, right out of the coal fields. I coached Mike as a freshman and saw that he really had all it takes to make a great football player. He now coaches prep football in a suburb of Chicago and we see one another occasionally at football dinners. Mike likes to remind me how poor we were at Duquesne; how the footballs we used in practice looked like watermelons. "Then one day, you came out with a new football," he tells me, "and I asked if I just could feel it, because I knew as a freshman I'd never get to play with it." That was Duquesne.

I left Mike behind when I left Duquesne as well as many other personal friends in the Pittsburgh area. It had been a wonderful seven years of association with some fine players, a great faculty and a loyal alumni.

CHAPTER ELEVEN

The weather in South Bend, Indiana in February 1934 was cold. So was the athletic climate. Many schools in the Big Ten had no ambition to play Notre Dame. For a variety of reasons, relationships had deteriorated. The university had a brand new stadium that was not being filled as often as we would have wished. The Depression made it hard to fill any stadium.

I had a lot of things to do when I arrived. The first job was to pick a staff. To begin with, I needed a secretary. He turned out to be Bob Cahill, who worked his way through school as my secretary. Bob joined me and stayed with me till I left seven years later. He then became the university's ticket manager and, with time out for World War II, has served in that capacity ever since. Herb Jones*

* Herb Jones died early in 1969 and was succeeded as business manager by Bob Cahill.

was the ticket manager when I arrived and later became business manager, a post he still holds. Art Haley held it when I came to the campus and after Herb moved up, Art moved on to the job of public relations director of the university. Joe Petritz was the publicity director who greeted me and he, too, stayed as long as I was coach. The next time I ran into Joe, he was publicity director for the All-America Conference, the rival of the NFL, of which I was then commissioner. Even so, we never let that get in the way of our friendship, just as it never bothered my relations with Jimmy Crowley, when he was commissioner of the All-American Conference.

A major task confronting me at Notre Dame was putting together a staff of assistant coaches. It had become customary for assistant coaches to leave along with the head coach. Back at Duquesne my only assistant was Joe Bach, and he had been elevated to head coach. Now it was up to me to put together a new crew of helpers. I like to think that I came up with just the right blend of the old and the new. To begin with the old, I signed up Chet Grant as backfield coach. Chet's playing days coincided with the George Gipp era of fourteen years earlier. After leaving college, Chet had drifted into semi-pro baseball and later sports writing. He was writing sports for the South Bend *Tribune* when I tapped him as an assistant, and this came as quite a surprise to folks close to Notre Dame football. Chet left Notre Dame with me, only to return a few years ago to put together an archive on books about sports for the university's new library.

Moving from the old to the new, I picked Tom Conley[*]

[*] Johnny O'Brien was next after Tom became head coach of

94

as my end coach. Tom had been captain of the 1930 team, the last one Rockne coached.

I went back to the Four Horsemen era for my other two assistants: Joe Boland and Bill Cerney. Boland had played behind Joe Bach at tackle on the 1924 team and had moved up to the first string in his senior year, 1925. He was my line coach and a very good one at that. He later became a well-known broadcaster of Notre Dame football games, operating out of WSBT in South Bend.

Bill Cerney had played behind me at fullback all through my Four Horsemen days. Bill liked to be billed as "The Fifth Horseman." While thumbing through old clippings to refresh my memory, I ran across a story printed in the South Bend *Tribune* on the occasion marking the twenty-fifth anniversary of the Four Horsemen. It began: "Outlined against a gray-blue November sky, the Fifth Horseman rode the bench again today," and it was about Bill Cerney. The author of the piece was, to my amazement, Ed Snyder, who has helped me write this book.

Now that I had a staff and a secretary, I called in the players, one by one, to meet them, to get acquainted and, most of all, to find out how they were doing in their studies. To my shock, one of my stars, Bill Shakespeare was having trouble with English.

The subject of grades had taken on new importance because Father O'Hara had decided that the advent of a new coach was the right time for some new athletic eligibility rules. Until then, a player only had to maintain a passing average. Father O'Hara felt that Notre Dame

---

John Carroll University in Cleveland. Johnny was killed in an automobile accident and Joe Benda succeeded him as end coach.

athletes should maintain a better than passing average. He decreed that to be eligible for football, a player not only had to pass all of his subjects; he also had to maintain a 77 average, which was seven points above the passing mark. Quite honestly, I did not favor this change. When I got word of it, I called in Bob Cahill, who knew his way around the university's record offices, and gave him a list of eight distinguished alumni of the university. These ranged from bank presidents to railroad presidents. "Bob, go over and find out just what kind of averages these gentlemen had," I told him.

I had the notion that if I could show Father O'Hara that some of his best contributors had less than a 77 average, he might relent.

Bob Cahill reported the next day that all the names on my list had averages in the 80's or better. "And while I was there, Mr. Layden," he added, "I checked your average and I might say you were lucky that this rule wasn't enforced ten years ago."

Father O'Hara had another rule change for me. He decreed that a player would be eligible for only eight semesters of college competition. Until then, transfer students often competed in sports for considerably more than eight semesters, particularly if they were good players. He wisely pointed out that he expected the Big Ten to change the same rule and, since Notre Dame followed Big Ten eligibility requirements, he wanted to be ahead of the game for a change. He was right. Shortly afterward, the Big Ten did change.

The 77 average rule remains in force at Notre Dame. I was the first Irish coach to live with it, and I trust my successors have found it as easy as I finally did. I can't remember losing a single outstanding boy because he couldn't make the average. I will confess that a few did give me a few anxious moments, but it all worked out for the best.

Here I should emphasize that the conditions for an athletic scholarship at Notre Dame had not changed in the nine years I had been away. Athletes still had to work at a part-time job to qualify and, to my consternation, a good many of my players were doing just what I had done—waiting on table in the student dining hall. Until World War II, a student at Notre Dame dined in the presence of waiters, or, if he were a working guy, waited in the presence of diners. The war ended that and brought in the cafeteria system. During my seven years as coach, I carried on a running battle with the dining hall bosses whose schedule for waiters determined how long I could carry on a practice session.

We also, of course, had boys on the team who were paying or working their own way through school without the benefit of any athletic scholarships. One was Jack Robinson, the center on my first team at Notre Dame and the first boy I coached there who was picked as an All-American. Once Jack made the first team, I saw that he was put on scholarship. I had several other players who moved on to scholarships the same way. One famous case I can remember is that of Dick McKenna, a fourth string quarterback about whom you'll hear later.

One player already under scholarship on my arrival was Francis Louis Layden, otherwise known as Mike, my kid brother. Mike had starred at Davenport High School

97

and caught the eye of Charlie Weiman, the president of John Deere Company in neighboring Moline, Illinois. Mr. Weiman, a loyal alumnus of Yale, decided Mike should go there, and to beef him up academically for the Ivy League underwrote a year at Milford Prep School for my younger brother. Meanwhile, Jesse Harper and Hunk Anderson visited me after a Notre Dame game in Pittsburgh and asked if I would intercede for the old alma mater and try to talk Mike out of Yale. This, I told them, I could not do. Apparently, they got to him with a stronger pitch than Yale because when I arrived on the Notre Dame campus, Mike was in his junior year.

During his last two years in college, I bent over backwards not to give the slightest inkling of favoritism. I was doing this in spite of the advice of my father, who during Notre Dame football season, frequently managed to visit my sister in South Bend; not only seeing the games, but dropping by at practice sessions. I'll never forget his advice:

"Elmer," he said, "if you want a winning team, play your ten best men and your brother."

My players all liked dad, especially those who had been injured and were in need of therapy. Dad's idea of therapy was taking such a boy out for dinner that was accompanied by a few beers and, in the case of non-beer drinkers, something even stronger. I didn't mind him taking a boy to dinner. I drew the line on the beverages that were served. I finally reached a point where my first advice to an injured player was: "Stay away from my dad."

We were dogged by more than injuries during those first few years at Notre Dame. We also suffered by the death of two of our players. John "Tex" Young, who would have been one of our first team halfbacks, died of a blood infection during the summer vacation in 1934. Then in March 1935, Joe Sullivan, a fine tackle and captain-elect of the 1935 team, died from the complications of pneumonia. The 1935 team kept Joe's memory alive throughout that season, dedicating each game to him. We didn't elect a new captain, but appointed a different player to act as captain for each game.

Bill Smith, a guard, was elected captain of the 1936 team, and I began to wonder if my captains were jinxed when a pre-season operation forced Bill to quit football and resign his captaincy. John Lautar, another guard, was elected to be acting captain for that season.

We also lost some great supporters among the faculty. Father Charles O'Donnell, the president when I had been hired, succumbed to a long illness. He had been in a hospital in Florida when I took Duquesne to play in the Festival of Palms, and I had visited him there to get his blessing as his new athletic director and head football coach. The occasion was New Year's Eve and I had done a bit of partying with Tom O'Neal, an alumnus, and his wife before visiting the hospital. Looking back, I was probably rather brash for visiting my new boss with a hint of spirits on my breath, yet Father O'Donnell was most kind and hospitable.

Another great supporter among the Holy Cross priests was Father John Cavanaugh, the elder, as he later became known to differentiate him from a younger Father John Cavanaugh, who served as president of the university from 1946 to 1952 and also acted as technical consultant on the Knute Rockne All-American movie. The older Father John had been president during Rock's rise to glory and was a devout football fan. When I arrived at the campus, he was in his last illness and I visited him on occasion at the hospital. One evening, during one of our last visits together, he turned to me and said, "Elmer, how about a snort?"

"A snort?" I exclaimed.

"Sure. There's a pint under the blanket on the top shelf of that closet," he told me.

And so we toasted one another and the future football fortunes of Notre Dame. These fortunes in my first season were not as good as I would have liked them to be.

We opened the 1934 season with Texas. Texas had a new coach, Jack Chevigny, who the season before had been an assistant to Notre Dame coach Hunk Anderson. Jack, who died fighting with the Marines in World War II, went down in Notre Dame history as the guy who scored the touchdown that "Won one for the Gipper." That was in the 1928 upset over Army when Rock gave a famous half-time speech about George Gipp's dying wish; that someday when the chips were down and things were going against the team, he hoped Rock would ask them to go out and win one for the Gipper.

Well, on the game that marked my debut as Notre Dame's head coach, Jack went out and won one for Chevigny, a big one for him because, as I recall, he went on to be named coach of the year in 1934.

The final score was only 7-6 in Texas's favor and later one critic claimed we would have won had I not played practically every member of my team. To this, I could only respond that a coach only can get to know what his players can do by letting them play. Furthermore, I always felt that a coach owes it to his team to let as many play as possible. Nobody wants to practice all week and then spend the game on the bench.

Pittsburgh and Navy also beat us that season. In turn, we beat Purdue, Carnegie Tech, Wisconsin, Northwestern, Army, and Southern California.

We also brought off a trick play, one that became known as our "talking play." It worked like this: Bud Bonar, our quarterback, began to call signals, the fullback would call out, "check," Bud then would walk back to the fullback as if to straighten out the signal. As he walked back the ball was snapped to the halfback and our opponent was supposed to be caught flat-footed. We tried it against Northwestern and it worked for a touchdown. But like all trick plays, it never worked again. Word had gotten around about Notre Dame's "talking play."

Our basic offense remained the same as under Rock: the T-formation with the Rockne shift into what was called the Notre Dame box. In the box formation, a halfback and the fullback are set deep; the quarterback and another halfback are set up close to the line.

We did change Rock's basic defense. Rock had favored the 7-1-2-1 formation. We switched the team to the 6-2-2-1. You rarely see either anymore. Most college teams today favor a 4-4-3 or a 5-3-2-1. Since this is not meant to be a technical discussion of football, I won't venture an explanation of any of these defensive tactics.

Just let me say that when I lost my first game as Notre Dame's coach, I also heard static about tampering with Rock's old defense.

What did we stress at practice? The fundamentals are what we stressed, blocking and tackling. You can cook up all the fancy plays you want as a coach, but they won't amount to anything unless your boys can block and tackle. I've yet to meet a successful college coach who didn't operate this way.

We stressed the fundamentals and by our second season this strategy, if you can call it that, began to pay off.

CHAPTER TWELVE

An old friend once described my coaching career at Notre Dame this way: "Elmer, you may never have had an undefeated season, but you certainly coached an all-time number of cliff-hangers."

By cliff-hangers, he meant games that were not decided until the closing minutes, and now that I check back over the records, I think he was right. The athletic publicity department at Notre Dame puts out a football guide each fall that dates back to the first game the school ever played. It makes a point of listing close games that were decided within the last five minutes. After checking it over, I think I hold the modern record for cliff-hangers with nine of them in my seven years of coaching.

If ever there was a year of the cliff-hanger, it was 1935,

and if ever there was a cliff-hanger that beats them all it was our 1935 game with Ohio State.

I still like to think that this was the most exciting college football game ever played. When sportswriters were polled in 1951 to pick the most thrilling football game of the first half of the twentieth century, they chose the 1935 Ohio State-Notre Dame game. This was the game that taught Hollywood writers how to put a thrilling finish to the rash of 1930's movies about football. It was a game that most of the Hollywood scriptwriters would not have dared to dream up. It was too unbelievable to be true.

Before we get to the game itself, let me tell you a little background.

One of the first games I scheduled after becoming athletic director of Notre Dame was with Ohio State. L. W. St. John was the athletic director there and we agreed to a home and home series for 1935 and 1936, The 1935 game was scheduled for November 2 in Columbus, Ohio; the 1936 game for Notre Dame Stadium.

Meanwhile, Ohio State had hired a new coach, Francis Schmidt. He had arrived on the Buckeye campus the same year I had arrived at Notre Dame. He came with a most successful record as coach of Texas Christian University. Were he alive today, he would be considered way ahead of his time. At the time he arrived in Columbus, he was light years ahead of the times. One of his former players has told me that he taught them 300 different plays running out of seven different basic formations. By today's standards, that is pro teaching and it takes a smart bunch of pros to learn it all. By 1935 standards, that was real "razzle dazzle," the name given to Schmidt's style of play where one, two and even three lateral passes might be made on a single play. Schmidt lived, ate, and slept football. He was as absorbed in the game all his waking hours as some recent fans think Vince Lombardi was when he coached Green Bay.

Like all coaches, Schmidt had to attend a full measure of banquets where they say he spent his time diagraming plays on the tablecloth until it was his turn to talk. A famous story about him was the time he was on his way to a banquet and had car trouble. He pulled the car into a garage and had it hoisted up over the grease pit. While the mechanic was inspecting the underside of the car, Schmidt concentrated on football. All of a sudden, still talking to one of his assistant coaches, he opened the door and fell eight or ten feet into a grease pit.

Francis Schmidt was the coach we faced November 2, 1935. He brought an undefeated team into the game, a team that was being touted for not only the Big Ten title, but also the national championship. The week before they played us, Schmidt's team had nearly demolished the University of Chicago.

At Notre Dame, the team already had one cliff-hanger under its belt for the year. We had no trouble getting by Kansas, Carnegie Tech, or Wisconsin. Then we met Pittsburgh, still coached by that famous dentist, Dr. Jock Sutherland. Jock had administered a painful 19-0 defeat to us the year before and we were out for revenge. Yet it took us until the last three minutes to beat him, 9-6. The winning margin was a field goal kicked by our end, Marty Peters, the first field goal he ever tried at Notre

Dame and one that at the last second was blown by a blessed wind between the uprights. With that wind earlier, Bill Shakespeare had gotten off a punt that traveled nearly 90 yards from our end zone and had given us the momentum to later score our only touchdown. This was the only time we beat Pitt during the four times we played them in my Notre Dame days. Harking back to my Duquesne days, it was the only time I ever coached a team that beat Jock Sutherland.

We had one more game before Ohio State, with Navy in Baltimore, and we won that, 14-0.

We were unbeaten; so was Ohio State. The stage was set for what was billed to be the game of the century and turned out just that way. Ohio State had sold out its stadium, which then seated slightly more than 81,000 people. In a depression year, this was quite a feat. Perhaps it wasn't in Columbus, where football had become almost a way of life. Newspaper writers had forced extra seats into the press box and converged on both campuses to begin the build-up.

At our campus, we were having our usual problems getting the team in shape to play. Two players were getting particular attention: Wally Fromhart, a quarterback, and Andy Pilney, a halfback.

Wally was my extra point kicker and he hadn't done as well as I would have liked in the earlier games. I decided to give him some special instruction on how to set his feet during a place kick to get better results.

Andy was in his senior year. He had come to school highly recommended and had shown flashes of brilliance as a runner. Yet he always seemed to be a half jump ahead of himself. In the open field, he was magnificent, but to get to the open field, he had to get through a hole in the line and still hold onto the ball. Andy had been plagued with stumbles and fumbles. Chet Grant had been working with Andy, and in the Navy game, he had run back some punts that had set up our touchdowns. Chet had taught Andy how to catch the ball on the run and he had learned his lessons well. He had been a big factor in our Navy victory, and now all of us had high hopes for him.

Lest Andy let his recent achievements cause his head to swell, I tried a little psychological warfare. Its name was "Bearskin."

During Rock's days as coach, he would write an occasional column for the South Bend *Tribune* under the heading of "Bearskin" in which he would deflate any egos that he felt needed deflating. I resurrected the idea of this column when I came in as coach and, with Joe Petritz, our publicity man, would turn out an occasional "Bearskin" column during the season. We took on Andy in "Bearskin" as the halfback with the biggest scrapbook of clippings on the team.

We also waged psychological warfare on the team in general. We were the soul of pessimism when writers visited us during the week before the game. We were ready to agree that Ohio State had a much better team; that the most we could hope for was holding down the score. We brought this attitude of gloom to a peak on the day before the game when our team arrived in Columbus. Local writers got me aside and asked for a prediction. "We'll be lucky to hold Ohio State to 40 points," I told

107

them. One afternoon newspaper printed that quote across the top of page one.

The team was quartered for the night at St. Charles Borromeo Seminary outside Columbus. For many years, we put up at such retreats because they were quiet as well as reasonable in cost.

All I sent to the team that night in the way of encouragement was a stack of Columbus newspapers bearing the headline that we would be lucky to hold Ohio State to 40 points. History shows that this was a fine way to get a team "up" for a game.

Reading later accounts, I learn that there was a carnival atmosphere in Columbus that night. Hotels had cleared the lobbies of furniture, and local bars had taken in extra stock. Since I never got back to Columbus for a game, I don't know for sure if this evening was any different. I had little chance to join the carnival, if there was one, because I was booked to appear at a smoker attended by officials of both schools and leading citizens. A highlight of this affair was the mayor of Columbus giving me the key to the city, then taking it back afterward so he could use it again. Obviously, he figured we were losers and he didn't want to waste a key.

Joe Petritz tells of doing the town with a midwestern sportswriter who became so indignant at hearing how bad we were going to be beaten the next day that he phoned his wife, ordered her to draw some money from the bank and place it with a bookie the next day on Notre Dame. Our breathtaking finish left him with hands shaking so bad that he could hardly write his story, Joe says.

While Columbus was having pre-game revelry, a train pulled out of South Bend carrying those students who could afford a train ride and a ticket to the game. Each year, there was a student trip and the Ohio State game had been selected for 1935. A few of our players also were on this train. We only carried forty players on trips. That was all we were permitted. But when a boy could pay his own way on the student trip and was willing to carry along his own uniform, we welcomed him to join us on the bench. That way he didn't have to buy a ticket. Among the handful of players on the student trip, lugging his uniform for his ticket of admission, was Dick Mc-Kenna, our fourth string quarterback. When he arrived at the stadium, he had a devil of a time getting the guards to find one of our student managers to let him into our dressing room. Lucky for us he did get in, because as it turned out, he was the most needed player that afternoon.

Now for the game itself. The first half was all Ohio State. About the only luck we had was winning the toss of the coin. We received, got nowhere on three downs, and Shakespeare got off a magnificent punt deep into Ohio territory. Four downs later, he returned an Ohio punt to midfield and it seemed like we might have a scoring drive about to begin. But on the first play, my brother Mike's pass was intercepted by Frank Antenucci, the Ohio fullback, on his own 30. He then executed a classic Francis Schmidt play, a play that Schmidt had in fact written about in a magazine article months before. Antenucci ran five yards or so, then got off a 10-yard lateral to Frank Boucher along the sidelines. Boucher had a wall of blockers ahead of him and went the next 65 yards for a touchdown. Dick Beltz kicked the extra point and the Buckeyes were ahead, 7-0.

Stan Pincura, the Buck quarterback, intercepted another pass of ours in the second quarter and from this launched a drive that brought Ohio its second touchdown. One of the plays in this scoring drive involved a double lateral pass and that really left the crowd in awe of Schmidt's razzle-dazzle. Ohio missed the point after, and we went to the dressing room behind, 13-0.

A few favored alumni always seemed to manage to work their way into the Notre Dame dressing room, and there were a few waiting in our quarters expecting to hear a Rockne-style pep talk before the second half began. While we didn't have a Gipper, we did have a Joe Sullivan and besides, this was November 2, marked throughout Catholicism as All Soul's Day, a day set aside for special prayers for the dead. I'm afraid I let these old grads down. If anything, I felt my team needed settling down, not pepping up. We had bad breaks in the first half and we had made some mistakes. As calmly as possible, I tried to discuss what we hadn't done right and should correct in the thirty minutes we had left. As a clincher, I said, "Gaul's team will start the second half."

Frank Gaul quarterbacked our second team. Pilney was playing halfback with that unit this day. The announcement stunned some of my first team players.

Until the closing minute, the third quarter was a see-saw punting duel. Then Pilney caught an Ohio punt on our 40 and, showing his great open-field running skill, took it back to the Ohio 13. After a line play failed,

Pilney passed to Gaul on the one-yard line for a first down. The next play, Steve Miller carried it over. It was time for Wally Fromhart to show the place kicking trick that I taught him. He took out a good sized divot, but missed the point.

Back down the field we came in the fourth quarter and fumbled at the goal line. Only three minutes were left when we got the ball again on our own 21. Two plunges gained us only four yards and Pilney faded to pass on the 10. Fromhart, now a catcher rather than a kicker, pulled it in on the Ohio 38. Three plays later we scored on a pass from Pilney to my brother Mike. Again Fromhart stepped back to kick what could be the tying point. The pass from center was not good and Wally kicked the ball into the center of the Ohio line. We still were behind, 13-12, and less than two minutes were left on the clock.

Our strategy was to try an onside kick, where you just boot the ball across the 10-yard neutral zone and try to recover before the opposing team can lay its hands on the ball. Ohio State expected just such a play and got the ball at mid-field. Ninety seconds were left. Ohio State had the ball and, barring some kind of miracle, our comeback was over.

One widely told story is that my wife was sitting up in the stands near Father O'Hara, who took this moment to console her by saying, "Don't worry, Edythe, Elmer and his boys have done a fine job." To which she is supposed to have replied, "That's easy for you to say. Your job doesn't depend on it."

One thing that did happen was that we lost telephone communication with Joe Boland, who was spotting for us

111

in the press box. Afterwards, someone suggested that maybe Ohio State had decided to tap our line in those closing seconds. I doubt that. It made no difference anyway. A wave of telepathy had been set up between Joe and me, or so it seemed to Chet Grant who was on the field end of the phone. Chet recalls that as he ran to me with each play Joe suggested, he would hear me just finishing sending that play into the game with a new quarterback.

Back at the 90-second mark, Ohio made the mistake of trying an end run. Dick Beltz was swarmed under by our boys. The ball squirted out of his hands and Hank Pojman, our second string center, touched it just as it rolled out-of-bounds. Time was out. It was our ball on our own 45. I sent in Gaul with a pass play. Pilney faded, saw his men covered and decided to run. Five tacklers had a shot at him and missed. Finally three Buckeyes crushed him out-of-bounds on the Ohio 19-yard line. Again the clock was stopped and so was Andy Pilney. That run ended his playing career. His leg was seriously injured, and we had to call for a stretcher to carry him off the field.

Shakespeare replaced Pilney and I sent Andy Pupilis, my third string quarterback, in with a pass play. Fifty seconds to play. Shakespeare faded, threw the ball and it bounced in and out of the arms of Ohio's Beltz. For a fleeting second, it looked like an interception. Time out again because of the incompleted pass. Second down, 19 yards and forty seconds to go. And I was out of quarterbacks. No, I wasn't. Chet Grant ran up pulling Dick McKenna with him. I gave McKenna a play we called a reverse pass where the ends cross each other's path and head in opposite directions. Again Shakespeare faded and threw. Wayne Millner leapt in the end zone, grabbed in the ball, and we were ahead, 18-13.

Sure, we missed the extra point. We kicked off again and Ohio had time for one desperate pass before the gun sounded. In less than two minutes, we had scored two touchdowns.

Francis Schmidt raced across the field and shook my hand as if he had won rather than us. I admit I was rather numb from those last two minutes, but I will never forget his graciousness.

Up in the press box, they say, pandemonium broke loose. Francis Wallace, a Notre Dame alumnus who was covering the game, tells in one of his books how he danced in circles with Bill Cunningham, a Boston sportswriter. Later he asked Cunningham, who was Dartmouth alumnus, why he had been so excited. "I'd just learned over the wire that Dartmouth had beaten Yale for the first time in years," Cunningham told Wallace.

Red Barber was broadcasting the game and recounted in later years how our Notre Dame spotter ran screeching from the radio booth after that final touchdown, and it took Red ten minutes to find out which of our ends had caught the winning pass.

One thing that many people who were there remember is that the crowd sat stunned. It did not push for the exits. It just sat stunned. It couldn't believe what had happened. Some of the people are said to have lingered as long as thirty minutes, perhaps wondering if there would be a recount.

An often-told fable is about the drunk leaving the game and running into another drunk who was just coming into the stadium.

"How is the game?" asked the second.

"The first three quarters are great, but don't stay for the fourth," said the other.

An old friend from a little town in northern Ohio tells how the Catholic ladies in his block bet their Protestant neighbor ladies that Notre Dame would beat Ohio State. After the thrilling finish, they paraded off to church to thank the Lord for this great Catholic victory.

"Little did they know," he said, "that the winning pass, Shakespeare to Millner, was pulled off by two Protestants."

And so it was.

CHAPTER THIRTEEN

If I were giving titles to these chapters, this one would be: "After the cliff-hanger comes the fall."

We were riding high after the Ohio State game. The newspapers still were recounting how it all happened in the last seconds at Columbus, how the team really lived up to its fight song that "what though the odds be great or small, old Notre Dame will win over all." For a week at least, we were the toast of the country's college football teams.

Then Northwestern visited us in South Bend. Northwestern had a new coach that season, Lynn Waldorf, and, over the years, I have had one bit of advice for every entrenched coach: beware of those newcomers. Northwestern had played Notre Dame fourteen times since 1889 and had won only once, in 1901 by the score of 2-0. It had pulled off a couple of ties during the intervening years, but it was not considered to be a powerful or frightening opponent.

By the end of the afternoon, it had pulled off the upset of the week, beating us, 14-7, and helping pave the way for Lynn Waldorf to be named "coach of the year" for 1935.

It should be noted in passing, that the winning touchdown in that game was an event to thrill the heart of any English teacher. Northwestern had a player named Longfellow, who pulled in the winning pass behind our Bill Shakespeare.

Our next game was with Army and it provided us with the third thrilling finish of the season. Army outplayed us most of the game and led, 6-0. We tied the score with twenty-nine seconds to play. We missed the extra point, and so the game ended in a tie. After the gun, Shakespeare, who was game captain that day, wrestled the game ball away from the Army team and presented it to me. I thanked Bill and walked across the field, where I presented the ball to Don Shuler, who was captain of Army. "You outplayed us most of the day, the ball belongs rightfully to your team," I told him.

I did not consider this to be any sort of grand gesture; just the sort of thing you'd expect any sportsman to do. Well, like many of the nice things you try to do in life, this gesture really paid off. Mrs. Shuler, the boy's mother, sent our team the biggest box of chocolate fudge I had ever seen as her way of repaying our little effort at sportsmanship. Don's father was a minister and he wrote the most glowing letter I ever received during my years of coaching. This was something I had forgotten until Bob Cahill reminded me that the *New Yorker* magazine picked me for its 1935 Sportsman of the Year award. I bring this up not by way of bragging, but merely to remind today's generation of football players and fans that sportsmanship still has a big place in the game.

If there was any team we owed the greatest measure of fame to, it was Army. Dating back to 1913, Army had been a fixture on our schedule and had helped us establish a reputation among fans in the East. During every single year I coached at Notre Dame, our game with the Army in Yankee Stadium was a sellout, a fact that brought joy to the heart of our business manager. Bill Wood coached Army during most of those years and together we came up with another idea: bringing our teams together for lunch the day before the game. Notre Dame and Army both had student bodies that came from all parts of the country. Why couldn't they be of help to one another in later years? So each Friday before the game, we'd bring the two squads together for lunch to get acquainted and talk about everything but football. From this practice stemmed many a friendship among our boys after they had left school.

We played Ohio State again in 1936, this time on our home field before a capacity crowd of 55,000, the first capacity crowd one of my teams had produced in the home field. Herb Jones, who was then ticket manager, said wistfully, "Why didn't we play them in Columbus where we could have sold 81,000 seats?" We beat the Buckeyes, 7-2.

We filled the stadium again for the Northwestern game that year. This time Waldorf's boys were favored and we upset them, 26-6.

We took our lumps, too. Pitt gave us a sound 26 to 0 beating and Navy upset us, 3 to 0. We also had a tie with Southern Cal.

The 1937 season ended the same way: six wins, two losses, one tie. The tie was with Illinois, which I had gotten back on our schedule. Pitt beat us again and Carnegie Tech upset us, 9 to 7. Minnesota also made its first appearance on our schedule and we upset the Gophers, 7 to 6. We also had a pair of cliff-hangers with Navy, where we won in the last two minutes, and with Southern Cal, where we scored the winning touchdown with one minute and forty-five seconds to play.

Pitt beat us again, once more powered along by a great halfback named Marshall Goldberg, who for a fleeting moment a few years earlier had been destined to come to Notre Dame. This was the year of Pitt's famous, dream backfield of Chickenero, Goldberg, Cassiano, and Stebbins as well as the year when it went to the Rose Bowl. Our other loss was an upset by Carnegie Tech.

The very best season I had at Notre Dame was in 1938. We won our first eight games, then had two weeks to get ready for the last one with Southern Cal. Aside from our opening game with Kansas, all of them had been tough, close games. Five of them had been sellouts. We arrived in Los Angeles being hailed as the prime candidate for national champions. The Los Angeles Coliseum was filled to capacity with 104,000 people, the largest crowd we ever played before, and the sixth sellout of our season. And we lost, 13-0.

A key play in that game, and one that was hashed over during the months afterward, came late in the second quarter. We had the ball with fourth down and six yards to go on our own 40-yard line. Bob Saggau, a former Iowa high school star and a great halfback, dropped back to punt. Instead of kicking, however, he ran with the ball and got within one step or two of breaking away for at least a first down and quite possibly a touchdown. Unfortunately, the gamble didn't work. Southern Cal had the ball in our territory and a few plays later scored on a pass. Steve Sitko, our quarterback, was criticized later for calling such a daring play. But Steve was not to blame at all. The play had been sent in from the bench. It didn't work. Nothing worked right that day.

Before leaving the 1938 season, there is one more play that stands out and bears recalling. We were playing Carnegie Tech at home. Bill Kern was in his first season coaching there and had a highly rated squad. Late in the game, Tech had marched to our 40-yard line. There still was no score. The Tech quarterback asked one of the officials what down it was. The official said, "Third down." The quarterback thought it was fourth down, but why challenge the official. So he tried a running play that didn't get the necessary yardage for a first down. When the play was over, the official said, "Sorry, it was fourth down" and gave us the ball. Well, as you can imagine, this brought a storm of complaint from Kern. However, since officials are never wrong, we still had the ball and put together a drive that won the game, 7-0. At the end of the season, Carnegie Tech was invited to the Sugar Bowl and came up with a very unusual gesture. It selected this official, the one whose error had cost them the game with us, to be on the team of officials for the Sugar Bowl game.

My last two seasons in coaching, 1939 and 1940, would have been great successes if we only played six games, because each of those years we won the first six games. Unfortunately, we played nine games and lost two of the last three games each of those two years.

The principal culprit both years was Iowa, whose coach then was Dr. Edward N. Anderson, the same Eddie Anderson of old, but now with a medical degree. Each of these years, I asked myself, "Why didn't Eddie stick with medicine instead of bothering with coaching?"

We played the 1939 game at Iowa City. This was the first time Notre Dame and Iowa had met since 1921 when the Hawkeyes upset Rock for the only loss of that season. Howard Jones coached Iowa to that victory. The captain of Notre Dame's losing team was Eddie Anderson. Now, in 1939, Eddie was in his first year as coach of Iowa. His team that year became famous as the "Iron Men" because most of them played just about every minute of every game. The star of the team was Nile Kinnick, who went on to win the Heismann Trophy as the outstanding player of the year. Kinnick was not only a great halfback, he was a magnificent kicker. He could drop kick extra points and punt with the best of them. It was Kinnick's extra point that beat us, 7-6, after we set up Iowa's touchdown by trying to run an intercepted pass out of our own end zone.

Guess who was picked as coach of the year for 1939? Yep, Eddie Anderson. I hardly missed a year when I didn't help make some newcomer coach of the year.

Iowa beat us again in 1940, this time, 7-0, in our own stadium.

From both games I drew criticism for my choice of starting halfbacks. Our left halfback generally carried the burden of passing and ball carrying. I also liked a half-back who could punt. I had two great left halfbacks in 1939—Harry Stevenson and Benny Sheridan. Harry was the best punter, a good passer, but a bit slow afoot. Benny was the shiftiest runner. The 1939 Iowa game was played on a clear, sunny day. I went most of the game playing Harry when my critics felt I should have played Benny. The next year, on a cloudy, windy, wet day, I went most of the way with Benny when my critics thought I should have played Harry.

Bob Cahill still likes to kid me about this choice. The first time the two of us ever sat in the stands together to watch a Notre Dame football game was in 1941 at Yankee Stadium where the Irish, under Frank Leahy, played a scoreless tie in the rain with Army. As the game ended, Bob turned to me and asked, "Who would you have played? Harry Stevenson or Benny Sheridan?" Both had been graduated by then, so Leahy did not have the choice.

My last game as a coach was on December 7, 1940 against Southern California in the Los Angeles Coliseum. We won that game, 10-7, and all ten points were scored by one man: Milt Piepul, our fullback. Over the years, it had become something of a tradition at Notre Dame to elect a lineman as team captain. The 1940 team broke this tradition by electing Milt Piepul. Milt ended his captaincy in a blaze of glory by doing all the scoring in his last game. This also was the last game coached by Howard Jones, who had beaten Notre Dame as coach of Iowa (that 1921 affair) and more recently had beaten me twice while coaching Southern Cal. Howard was one of the really fine men in football. One of his favorite boasts was that someday he'd beat Notre Dame by playing eleven Catholics against us. One year, he darn near did.

Another great coach was on our schedule in 1940, Amos Alonzo Stagg. We opened the season with College of the Pacific coached by Stagg. This game was played in South Bend the weekend they held the première of the movie, "Knute Rockne All American." How it came to be scheduled comes up next.

CHAPTER FOURTEEN

At Notre Dame, I wore two hats; one as coach, the other
as athletic director. If Coach Layden thought his schedule was too tough or he didn't get enough scholarships
for football players, he had only one fellow to blame, Athletic Director Layden. I was the last coach to wear both
hats during my Notre Dame stay. Frank Leahy, my successor, tried it for some years, then turned over the
athletic directorship to Edward W. "Moose" Krause, who
has continued in that job through several successors to
Leahy. Most colleges today recognize that each is a full-
time job in itself. Coaching and being boss of a college
athletic department have become too complex and time-
consuming for a single man to perform both duties well.
Furthermore, the job of athletic director calls for a high
degree of tact and diplomacy at all times, traits that some
coaches might find themselves lacking during moments

of stress. The coach deals primarily with young men; the athletic director primarily with older men who are on the same level in the academic scheme of things.

I like to think that I really worked at the athletic director's job. I certainly put in plenty of time at it. I tried to show up for every home athletic contest we had on the campus as well as intramural games between our student resident halls. In order to clean up all the paper work connected with the job, I spent many Sunday afternoons in my office dictating to Bob Cahill. Bob likes to tell about the Sunday I was so wrapped up dictating that I almost kissed him instead of my wife when she came to collect me for dinner. He had gotten up out of his chair when my wife walked into the office, being the gentleman that he is. I got up from the desk, walked around to the two of them and almost missed the proper target.

Joe Petritz, who was our publicity director, recalled those days with me not long ago and gave me what I consider to be a very fine compliment. "You know, Elmer," he said, "as an athletic director, you were like Harry Truman. History will prove you were great." I doubt that, but I appreciated the compliment.

One of the tasks I liked best was putting together schedules for our various teams. When I arrived in South Bend, Notre Dame needed some fence-mending in the Big Ten. Several schools in the Western Conference were not anxious to play us in any sport because, for some reason or another, they had crossed swords with Rock. While a great coach and a great person, Rock at times could cross somebody the wrong way. No successful person such as he was can be everything at the same time. At one time, the University had almost been a part of the Western Conference. As a student, I could remember taking part in a Big Ten track meet in 1922 at Michigan. Our eligibility rules were stricter than those enforced by the conference. We drew officials for our games from the same pool.

My friendly association among Big Ten schools, I feel, had some fine results. We scheduled Ohio State and Minnesota for the first time. We brought Iowa and Purdue back on the schedule. Our biggest triumph was getting Fielding Yost, the Michigan immortal, to visit our campus and agree to a home and home series that was played after I had left as coach. Meanwhile, we kept alive our valuable relationships with Army, Navy, Northwestern, Georgia Tech, Southern California, and Navy. Our relations with Navy were as fine as those with Army. Over the years we dealt with Andy McFall, Ike Giffin, Dave Brown and Pogue Smith to name a few of the Naval Academy athletic directors. All of them became admirals, I believe, as did many of the Middies who played against us.

Looking back, I would say that the best thing I had going for me in these schedule discussions was something my parents had taught me—be polite and considerate of your elders. I was only thirty-one when I arrived at Notre Dame, a boy compared with the older men who oversaw athletics at these other schools. While I didn't approach them as a boy with hat in hand, I did respect their greater experience and I can't think of anyone I met who didn't become a friend.

Another thing that helped was my being selected as a

member of the college coaches' rules committee by Mal Stevens of Yale, who was president of the coaches association. This brought me in contact with the top men around the country and opened many doors that otherwise would have been closed.

During my first few years at Notre Dame, I was invited to sit in on Big Ten schedule meetings in an unofficial capacity, of course.

Bo McMillen had moved to Indiana as coach and we talked about scheduling a series. Noble Kizer, my old teammate from 1924, was coaching Purdue and got wind of the deal. So first we put Purdue on the schedule and later Indiana was added; old teammates first, then a fellow coach from the Duquesne days.

One game that I really enjoyed adding to the schedule was with the College of the Pacific. The coach was Amos Alonzo Stagg, that grand old man of football who probably brought to the game more qualities of character than any other college coach in history. Remember, he was the fellow who invented the idea of the shift that Jesse Harper later brought to Notre Dame and Rock perfected. All of this was done at the University of Chicago, where Stagg became more famous than President William Rainey Harper, the man who founded the school with Rockefeller money and was its first president. The city named a street after Harper; the university named the field house after Stagg, and it reached its final prominence as the place where a group of scientists set off the first nuclear chain reaction that led to development of the atomic bomb.

The University of Chicago had retired Stagg. He and

Mrs. Stagg had been East to his 50th class reunion at Yale University. On the way back West to his new job at College of the Pacific, Stagg stopped by the Notre Dame campus. It was a soggy, hot day in August when he walked into my office with his tie off and his shirt collar open. He said he'd like to see if he could schedule a game with us. After some brief conversation, I found out that he had left Mrs. Stagg sitting in the car. I sent Bob Cahill to get her and ordered some cold lemonade for all of us. Then I phoned Father O'Hara to ask if he could spend a few minutes with this grand gentleman. He told me to bring the Staggs to his office. When we arrived he was sitting with Frank B. Hering, who had coached Notre Dame football before the turn of the century, but became better known as the man who invented Mother's Day. As we walked in, Hering jumped to his feet, walked over to Mrs. Stagg, took her hand in his and asked, "Mary, how have you been?"

It turned out that Frank Hering had dated Mrs. Stagg when both were youngsters.

Of course, we scheduled the game. No coach would have turned down Stagg, let alone a young athletic director who constantly appreciated the opportunity of associating with men like Yost of Michigan, Zuppke of Illinois, Bill Alexander of Georgia Tech, St. John and Schmidt of Ohio State, Wilson and Waldorf of Northwestern, Bill Hunter and Howard Jones at Southern Cal, Al Masters of Stanford and Frank McCormick of Minnesota just to name a few of the people who helped me give Notre Dame some of the toughest schedules a coach could ever hope to play.

From a practical standpoint, the athletic director has to put football first if he hopes to pay the way for other sports. His basketball team might break even on expenses if he's lucky. The other sports are run at a financial loss. Yet without the other sports, you are not offering the kind of varied athletic program that a college deserves. Every boy is not a football player, nor for that matter a football fan. At Notre Dame, we found interest in fencing and started that sport for the first time. We had a tennis team coached by a modern language professor, George Langford, and captained by a great guy named Bill Fay, who kept after us day in and day out to improve the tennis courts. Finally, we found enough money in the budget to do it.

We had some great basketball teams in my time, coached by George Keogan; fine baseball teams coached by Jake Kline, who also taught mathematics; a track team coached by John Nicholson that produced Greg Rice, the top two-miler of the 1930's as well as many other fine track men.

It also was our job to encourage intramural sports. The Rockne Memorial Field House was opened during my span as athletic director and dedicated specifically to intramural athletics. The only varsity team that could set foot inside the place was our golf team, which used the pro shop locker rooms since the field house was located next to the university golf course and contained the pro shop.

As the spokesman for Notre Dame's athletic program, I had the opportunity of traveling the country speaking to alumni groups, men's clubs, and various athletic banquets. It kept me away from home more than I should have been, yet it also introduced me to hundreds of wonderful people who kept Notre Dame in mind when they saw a boy who stood out in athletics. It once was said that no devout Catholic boy of athletic prowess could dare think of going to any college but Notre Dame. I wish this had been true, as do many Notre Dame coaches before and after me. The folks we met in our travels, however, proved to be good scouts in more ways than one, and certainly we needed every bit of help we could get when it came to recruiting.

CHAPTER FIFTEEN

When Father O'Hara laid down his new rules for football after I had arrived, he not only changed the eligibility requirements, he also changed the recruiting procedures. I was told that I was not to leave the campus to sign up any football prospects. If a boy wanted to see me, he was to come to the campus. If I wanted to see a boy, I had better make a novena that somebody would bring him to the campus to see me. At a time when aggressive coaches were chasing good prospects all over the countryside, I was tied to a chair hoping for my scouts of real and subway alumni to send me bright, athletic types. Father O'Hara did not say that I couldn't talk to a boy who approached me on the street or at some far-off banquet. His main rule was: don't approach them; make them approach you.

Like a legendary fisherman, the best stories I have to

tell about recruiting are about the "ones that got away."
Right at the head of the list goes Marshall Goldberg.
Can you imagine what it would have meant for today's
so-called ecumenical movement if Marshall Goldberg
had been an All-American at Notre Dame? Well, he was
an All-American, but at Pitt. Yet we had a crack at him.
Doc O'Donnell, my old friend from Duquesne days,
scouted Marshall and began telling him about the glory
of Notre Dame. Marshall's dad, who listened into this
discussion, was not opposed to the idea of his son attending what was a Catholic college. Mr. Goldberg, however, wanted to meet in person the man who would be
coaching his son. I was tied to a campus 500 miles away.
Jock Sutherland, on the other hand, was nearby and quite
probably came on stronger as the sort of stern leader
that appealed to Mr. Goldberg. He also had a slightly
better package to offer: everything we did, but no part-
time job to pay for it, as was still required of a Notre
Dame athletic scholarship.

The Marshall Goldberg story didn't leak out until Notre
Dame played Pitt in 1936 and Marshall scored several
touchdowns against us. Then the word got out that Layden had a crack at him. One story had it that I told Marshall he would never be a good football player. Another
had it that Notre Dame could not stomach a Goldberg.
Both were out-and-out lies. Until he was on the field
against us, I never saw the man. Until I had left college
coaching and become commissioner of the National
Football League, we never got to know one another personally. He was a great player and I would have loved
to have him play for me anywhere, anytime.

I can't leave the Marshall Goldberg story without telling about the time Harry Stuhldreher and the rest of the Horsemen were gathered in a hotel room hearing about the only time Harry ever walked in his sleep. It happened, Harry said, the night before his Wisconsin team played Pitt. Harry dreamt that Goldberg was on his way for a touchdown and that he, Harry, had run from the bench to tackle him. This apparently got him out of bed and he walked into a closet door and got a big egg on his head. "But did you tackle Goldberg?" asked Jim Crowley.

Another big player that got away was Tommy Harmon. He played high school ball in Gary, Indiana, and was wooed with great dilligence by one of our alumni in that area, Charles "Chick" Bader. Chick managed to bring Tommy to South Bend to meet me, but, after thinking it over, Tommy chose to go to Michigan. We also had a crack at Billy Hillenbrand, who later starred at Indiana.

One of the brightest high school stars of that era was in the Chicago area and I had the briefest meeting on record with him. He showed up with a lawyer who was acting as his agent. I was not used to talking with a boy's agent. I would talk to the boy or his dad, but never to some third party who was trying to make a deal for him. In less than 10 minutes, I had dismissed this star and his agent and, even though he became a fine college player, I never regretted it for a minute.

Personally, I was quite happy with the ones that didn't get away. Several of them became All-Americans. Some of them were still around after I left and became All-American later. Three I can think of, off hand, are Angelo Bertelli, Pat Filly, and Creighton Miller, all of whom were unanimous All-Americans in 1943—Bertelli as a quarterback, Filly as a guard, and Miller as a halfback.

I remember the first time I met Creighton Miller. I was speaking in Wilmington, Delaware, and his dad, Harry, who had starred at Notre Dame years earlier, brought his little boy Creighton up to meet me and said, "Here's a boy who will make you a famous coach."

"I'll bet," I said to myself and I was right. I wasn't coaching when Creighton made the varsity and helped make my successor famous. He later went on to become a lawyer and founded the National Football League Players' Association.

I never coached any player to be an All-American. I coached every player to do the best he could. As a coach, the kind of All-American I was looking for was an all-American student. With that kind of rating in class, you could be sure he would be around for the games on Saturday. And that's when they picked the all-American football players.

CHAPTER SIXTEEN

It came as quite a shock to everybody connected with Notre Dame football when I announced my resignation on February 4, 1941. I resigned to become the first commissioner of the National Football League. It was doubly surprising to many of my friends because they had the idea I was well on my way to becoming a Notre Dame institution, perhaps not on a par with Rockne, but on a level of my own. I had never encouraged any of my players to enter the pro game. Of course, I had not actively discouraged them either. However, I tried to point them toward coaching if they planned to stay in football, and many of them followed that direction and became fine high school and college coaches.

My stated reasons for leaving Notre Dame were the usual ones given by any employee to his boss when he finds a better job: more money, more security, a better life for his family. Behind these reasons was a matter of contract. When I came to Notre Dame, it was with a three-year contract. After two years had gone by, Father O'Hara ripped that up and gave me a five-year contract. This expired in February 1941. As it neared expiration, Father O'Hara was now Bishop O'Hara and Father J. Hugh O'Donnell was president of the university. When my new contract arrived, it was for one year only. I went to see Father O'Donnell and complained that I had come under longer terms and expected a contract with longer terms. He told me that he had decided to give nobody a contract for longer than a year, from the best professor and dean to the lowliest instructor, and this included the athletic director and head football coach. He then made the gesture of affixing his signature to the contract, handed it over and expected me to sign. I told him I'd have to think about it.

As I mulled the matter over, I recognized that some alumni probably were not happy about the fact that the Fighting Irish had not had an undefeated season under my regime. We had come close, but never quite made it. On the other hand, we were playing a much different brand of teams. Our schedule no longer was laced with pushover games. It was, in fact, about as tough a schedule as any college team was playing. It also included many Big Ten teams that the university dearly wanted to get on the schedule, not only for prestige but also for their drawing power at the box office. And the box office had been good during the past seven years.

There also was some grousing about the quality of our football material. A few of the alumni felt we didn't have .

136

the depth of talent that Notre Dame should expect. Here again, I had played the recruiting game by the book written by Father O'Hara. We were not scouring the country offering outside money and other side deals to promising players. All we could and did offer was a scholarship that required them to work at a part-time job. And then they had to come to see us, we couldn't go chasing after them in person. Finally, after they arrived, they had to maintain a better than passing average to remain eligible.

After giving a lot of thought to all of these things, I sought some outside advice. The late Arch Ward was sports editor of the *Chicago Tribune* and very close to the Notre Dame scene. I had come to know and respect Arch deeply. I set my problem before him and probably couldn't have made a better choice for an advisor.

Unknown to me at the time, the National Football League had decided that the time had come for it to have a commissioner. Baseball had Judge Kenesaw Mountain Landis, who had come to symbolize a rock of Gibraltar on which the name was based. When the judge spoke, baseball listened. So did the public. The judge had been hired after the 1919 Black Sox scandal to give the sport a respectable image, and he did that admirably well.

Professional football had a different problem. It was not faced with any scandal, it was faced with the problem of public acceptance. The sport of baseball drew millions of spectators. Professional football was lucky to play to a full stadium once or twice a season. The National Football League dates its founding back to 1921 and from then until 1939 it was headed by Joe F. Carr, who carried the title of league president. Carr labored long and hard during those years to get the game established and keep it flourishing. He died in May of 1939 and his job was passed along to Carl L. Storck, who had worked with Carr over the past eighteen years as a secretary-treasurer of the league. By the end of the 1940 season, some of the owners were beginning to feel that pro football should have a "football man" fronting for it. Two of them, George Halas of the Chicago Bears and Charlie Bidwill of the Chicago Cardinals, got together with Arch Ward to discuss the matter. Arch had given the professional game a major boost by instituting the All-Star Football Game in 1934. A year earlier, Arch had dreamed up the All-Star Baseball Game as an attraction for Chicago's Century of Progress world's fair. It had gone over so well that he came up with an All Star football game the next year, pitting a team of college stars who had graduated against the team that had won the previous year's National Football League title. The game was played in Soldier Field and drew upwards of 100,000, the kind of a crowd that made a pro owner's eyes bug. So Arch was a natural to discuss the commissioner situation with. In fact, Halas told me, that Arch was his and Bidwill's first choice for the job.

Arch turned it down, but suggested some other people as candidates. At this point, I came to him for advice on what I should do about Notre Dame. Our discussion ended with my name being added to the list of candidates for commissioner. Arch not only added my name, he pushed me enthusiastically with Halas, Bidwill, and the other owners.

On the second of February, 1941, I was in Chicago and signed a five-year contract to serve as commissioner of the league at $20,000 a year, nearly double what Notre Dame was paying me. We agreed to release the news of my new job on February 4, and I hurried back to South Bend to submit my resignation.

I had a full day to resign before the news hit and unfortunately it was a day when Father O'Donnell was not around the campus. The resignation lay on his desk all day. I began to get worried. I felt I owed it to him to let him know of my decision personally and not have him read about it in the newspapers.

Finally, at 8 o'clock at night, he returned and I received an immediate audience. He tried his best to talk me out of my decision, but, as I explained to him, "I thought long and hard about this before I made the decision. Furthermore, it will be hitting the papers very shortly."

Then he asked me to recommend a successor. My recommendation was Lawrence "Buck" Shaw, who had played with Gipp on the 1920 team and had gone on to become highly successful as coach of Santa Clara College. Buck not only was a good coach, he also was highly personable, the kind of guy who could keep the Notre Dame image bright and fresh in front of its friends across the country.

Father O'Donnell thanked me and a month later invited me over to his office to meet my successor: Frank Leahy.

Frank had been a tackle on the 1928 and 1929 teams but was sidelined by an injury in 1930. He spent that season on the bench watching Rock coach his last Notre

Dame team and he learned his lessons well. He did a fine job as line coach of Fordham under Jimmy Crowley. Then he moved to Boston College as the top man and had just had an undefeated season. Frank coached Notre Dame for eleven seasons and produced an .887 batting average in the won-lost column. Rock's average during his time was .897. Mine for seven years was .783. Of course, there's still a fellow named Ara Parseghian coaching Notre Dame and he is batting in the above .800 class at present. Even so, Frank will go down in history as one of the school's winningest coaches.

As I left Notre Dame, I promised myself I would never pipe off in public print about its football teams. As a former coach, as well as an alumnus, I vowed charity for my successors to follow. Well, I only broke that promise once. And it was Frank Leahy who prompted me.

Frank had retired from the Notre Dame scene in 1954. Terry Brennan succeeded him and in 1956 had a disastrous season. Going into the final game against Southern California, Notre Dame's season record was only two victories against seven defeats. On the eve of the final game, Frank popped off that the Fighting Irish had not only lost their fight, but also their will to win. That was too much for me, particularly after I was told that Frank's criticism stemmed from a personal disagreement with Terry over letting one of the Notre Dame players appear with Frank on a television show. So I popped off publicly at Frank to the effect that he was talking in poor taste; that he was publicity hungry, and, finally, tongue in cheek, "I guess Leahy has been away from

Notre Dame long enough to qualify as an expert, like I've become."

Since then I've kept quiet as both Frank and I probably should have done back in 1956. His taunts did nothing to help Notre Dame win its last game that year, nor did my rebuttal help Terry.

CHAPTER SEVENTEEN

Now that nearly thirty years have gone by and I read over my NFL contract again, I see that I was expected not only to keep peace among the owners, the coaches, the players, and the officials, but also work and pray to keep peace in the world. The contract, it turned out, had a war clause in it, even though it was drawn nearly a year before the United States entered World War II. Under this wartime provision, my $20,000 a year salary would be cut to $7,000 the first year that the league had to suspend operations because of a war and to $5,000 a year for the remainder of the contract after this suspension of play.

Before my first season had ended in 1941 we were in World War II, and I was mighty busy trying to keep the league from folding up. By now, my family had grown to a wife and four children and we were living in a house in Kenilworth, one of the North Shore suburbs of Chicago. Under the terms of my contract, I was to establish a league office, which I did in Chicago. I inherited Denny Shea who had become treasurer of the league and Shorty Raye, who had become the league's expert on rules. George Strickler soon joined us as my assistant and director of publicity for the league. While the league was solvent, it did not boast a large bank balance, so I was moved to help in every way I could to see that the money kept rolling in to the owners so we could support the league offices and meet the payroll: the secretary, Helen Nichin, Shea, Raye, Strickler, and me.

Of all this group, Denny Shea certainly had the most demanding job, trying to keep the league office afloat financially during the many months of cash drought each year. Across town, Judge Landis ran baseball without any financial worries. Professional football was not as fortunate. Only about half the teams made any profit at all; the rest operated at a loss. The commissioner's office had to depend on gate receipts and, until October each year, there were none, since all of the teams, except Green Bay, played in baseball parks where that sport kept them waiting until the end of September before they were allowed inside. There was no television, and each team peddled its own radio rights to its games. One of my first official acts as commissioner was to demand renegotiation of the radio rights for the NFL championship game. The network acted quite hurt that anybody had the nerve to try to get more money for airing a championship professional football game. When I read about today's TV deals that Pete Rozelle, the commissioner, has worked out, I almost want to drool.

Shorty Raye was not a full-time employee. George Halas had brought him onto the scene as a technical advisor to the commissioner before there was one. Shorty's forte was rules, and during his many years he brought about dozens of rule changes that made pro football the exciting, fast-moving game that it is today. Shorty's full-time job was as a schoolteacher. On the side, he was an official. At one time, he was the only man who was both a football, a basketball, and a baseball official in the Big Ten. Shorty's idea of attending a pro game was sitting with a stop watch and timing how long it took to get off a play and get ready for the next play.

One thing immediately caught his attention. When a play had ended, the official nearest the ball carried it in to the spot on the field where it would be placed or marked down. Why carry it? That takes time. Why not throw it to another official who was at the spot where the ball would be marked down? That was Shorty's reasoning, backed by several stop watch readings showing that the old practice wasted seconds. So one of the first changes during my time as commissioner was directing the officials to toss the ball to where it should be marked down for the next play.

Browsing through the latest NFL record book, I see that 1959 is noted as the first year since 1933 when the league did not make any rules changes. Most of the changes that were made can be traced back to the dogged analysis of the game that was made by Shorty Raye.

Recently, Halas and I were talking about the league and I was telling George of his great contributions to the sport of professional football. Modestly, George shrugged off what I had to say and told me, "The greatest contribution I've made was in the rules and I can only give Shorty Raye credit for most of them."

I managed to get through one rule change on my own. In 1945, I finally convinced the owners that their players should wear long stockings. I should make it clear that I did not run an athletic hosiery company. It was my feeling that the teams looked sloppy without long stockings. I felt it would save some bruises and cuts if they did and, just as importantly, cover up some awfully ugly legs. "Realize this," I told the owners, "your guys don't have legs like chorus girls."

We tried several other innovations. The down marker was changed from a four-sided device to a pole with flippers, more readable for quarterbacks. This change caught on and is used today throughout football. Another idea flopped: having each official wear a different colored shirt to indicate what his job was. Just like a judge might feel uncomfortable in anything but a black robe, the officials were uncomfortable without their striped shirts. And what a crowd of officials we had! They could make a book by themselves.

Irv Kupcinet was a growingly successful columnist for the *Chicago Times*. Today he is a highly successful columnist with the *Chicago Sun-Times*, runs a television talk show and does comment for the radio versions of the Bears games. Irv was just one of several newspapermen who moonlighted as NFL officials. In what may be

146

construed as bad public relations, I finally insisted that we keep newspapermen in the press box and out of striped shirts. I imagine a few of these reporter-referees grumbled, but the league seems to have survived.

We then had a big league baseball umpire who wintered in a striped shirt, Charlie Berry.

One of our most colorful officials was the famous Bobie Cahn. Bobie stood a regal five feet, two inches. His favorite stunt was jumping on top of a pile-up of players to retrieve the ball. How he survived in the company of the giant players we had then belies the imagination.

Ron Gibbs, Joe Lipp and John Schommer were other outstanding officials we had in the league.

Another great official who still is with the league in a supervisory job, was Bill Downes. Bill was and still is a real solid guy to have running a game. I don't imagine that the league ever had many complaints about his officiating. The only one I recall came from a lineman on the Chicago Bears who griped that Bill was the only official in the league who called fouls on him. After that, I instructed Bill and the other league officials to watch that particular Bear player closer. Bill and I still get together occasionally since he runs Chicago's airports.

Of course, the greatest characters in the National Football League were not the officials, nor the players, but the owners. What a crowd they were! I say they were, because only a few are left. Halas still runs the Bears and Art Rooney the Pittsburgh Steelers. George Preston Marshall had to give up running the Washington Redskins because of illness. Dan Reeves still runs the Rams, which, in my time, were based in Cleveland. Wellington

Mara and his sons have the Giants, but I dealt with their dad, Tim, not them. Curley Lambeau is gone from Green Bay; Fred Mandel from Detroit; Alexis Thompson from Philadelphia. Charlie Bidwill died the year after I left the commissioner's job, and his sons, Stormy and Bill now run what was the Chicago Cardinals in St. Louis. Ted Collins, who tried the sport in both Boston and Brooklyn, also is no more. Kate Smith, whom Ted is credited with bringing to the top in show business, still sings on as his greatest contribution to entertainment in America.

Whatever the owners ever write into league constitutions and job descriptions of commissioners, what each owner really wants is his own way. About the only time they come to complete agreement is when they decide to fire their commissioner. Lately, this has been shown in the case of major league baseball, where Judge Landis made the mold and nobody has fit ever since. Happy Chandler, Ford Frick, General Eckert have come and gone. None had a craggy face nor a mane of white hair.

I'm afraid I would never encourage a son or a grandson or anybody else for that matter to groom himself to be a commissioner for a professional sport. It doesn't matter what you do, or how well and zealously you try to do it, you are bound to step on some toes and these toes usually are attached to a team owner, who will begin planning to have you sacked.

During five years as the first commissioner of the NFL, I would tell myself repeatedly that, "After all, the owners made this league. They are putting up their money to make it go. How can I sit up on some lofty cloud and fire thunderbolts at them?"

The job was one of those situations where you were damned if you did and damned if you didn't. Your head was always out of the trench and everybody was shooting at you.

One leading marksman was George Marshall. George never came to a league meeting without his lawyer. George was not about to be without counsel once we closed the doors. We conducted our meetings under parliamentary procedure, and George wanted a guy with him who knew Roberts' Rules of Order.

Fortunately, time has dimmed my memory over many of the big hassles over small things that developed in these meetings. One still remains vivid and that was over the league schedule. We had the idea that we might help some of the financially-weaker teams if we could schedule them against teams with the bigger box office draw early in the season when the weather was still good. This way we hoped to lure out to the parks some new converts to the game. All went well until we tried to change the Green Bay-Bears game from the last Sunday in October to the end of November. We reasoned that a Bears-Packers game could draw under any and all weather conditions. We wanted to pit the Eagles against the Packers on that October date, hoping that good weather would shine on the game and convince some would-be Packer fans that the Eagles were a team worth watching. Over this one change, in a 52-game schedule, the schedule meeting dragged thirteen hours through the night, with the Bears protesting that the game traditionally had been played on the last Sunday of October and that any change would be downright detrimental to football. We finally gave up and agreed to leave tradition alone, but only after we got the Bears to indemnify the Eagles if the box office fell below a stated figure. It did, as we expected, and the Bears shelled out about $3,000, as I recall, to Bert Bell of the Eagles for failing to meet his box office goal.

The war, as expected, caused the league many problems. Cleveland suspended operations for one year. Pittsburgh and Philadelphia merged for one season, then Pittsburgh merged with the Chicago Cardinals for the next season. The league schedule was cut from fifty-five to fifty games and total attendance dropped under the million mark in both 1942 and 1943. Players were at a premium. The able-bodied were at war, leaving only a pool of over-aged and 4-F's for the teams to draw from. This situation resulted in one famous old-timer coming back to the game, the great Bronko Nagurski. Bronk had retired from the Bears after the 1937 season. Now in 1943, he was lured out of retirement and, as the great player that he was, thrilled 34,000 who watched the championship that year in Wrigley Field by scoring one of the Bears' touchdowns in their 41 to 21 victory over the Washington Redskins. The score was only 14-7 at half time, and George Marshall got so excited and eager to give his team a pep talk that he ran from the stands before the half ended and parked himself on the Bears bench for the last minute or so. This drew a howl of complaint from Ralph Brizzolara, who was running the club while Halas was in the Navy. Even though his players chased Marshall off their bench, I was urged to hit him with a stiff fine for this encroachment. I opted for a stiff reprimand instead and I'm afraid that Mr. Brizzolara still thinks I did the wrong thing.

Another wartime problem was travel. The Office of Defense Transportation had to be convinced that, while not vital to the nation's defense, pro football did deserve to get around the country to play its schedule. Fortunately, Colonel Eastman, whom we dealt with at ODT, happened to be a former pro football player who listened kindly to our arguments that the league deserved to be kept alive. Even so, we had to report regularly on what mode of travel each team took and how many miles were traveled by each.

Another important job performed by our office was keeping a list of college players eligible for drafting by the pro clubs. From the owners, I was able to obtain a policy statement that we would protect college players and college football in every way possible. We agreed to keep hands off college players with eligibility remaining until they had played out this eligibility. We recognized that the colleges were our minor leagues, so to speak, the best training ground possible for the pro game. We recognized also that the popularity of collegiate football could only rub off on the pro game if we did everything possible to enhance it. During the middle of the war, we went one step further and ruled high school players out-of-bounds for the professional draft. Unless there was some very serious extenuating circumstance, no high school player was to be deterred from entering college. As a result of this outspoken position, our relations with the colleges rose to a new high. The colleges knew they could count on the NFL to keep hands off their boys. Through the intervening years, professional football has stuck to this policy, and it has done the pro game a world of good.

As first commissioner of any professional sport, Judge Landis came to his job after a World Series betting scandal. Fortunately, the NFL had no betting problems flare up during my tenure, but I dealt with several red herrings of this type. The owners, or some of them, seemed to sniff a gambler under every locker room bench. During the season, I would get regular reports of various odds changes on upcoming games with worried plaints from one owner or the other to investigate.

Nevertheless, I went about the tracking down of any possible links between the betting fraternity and the players. I called on Judge Landis and asked him to tell me what baseball did to prevent betting by the players. The judge said the big leagues had no special program; that he investigated every rumor as it came up. Then I went to Washington and met with J. Edgar Hoover of the FBI to seek his advice. Mr. Hoover, who happens to be a great sports fan, told me his Bureau had not come across any hints of tampering with our players or our teams. Finally, I retained a firm of private investigators that was unable to turn up one shred of evidence of any links between our players and gamblers. This action was taken independent of the owners, yet in keeping with their mandate in my contract that I was to oversee the purity of the game. After leaving the league, I burned these reports because, in my opinion, they were valueless.

The league finally did have a betting scandal involving a championship game in the late 1940's. Bert Bell had become the commissioner and it was ironic that he should be the victim since during his days as an owner, he had

been the one who sent me the most alarms about suspected betting.

The event that really stunned the NFL was the advent of the All-America Conference. Again ironically,
the man behind the formation of this new league had been
one of the NFL's best friends—Arch Ward. Through the
Chicago Tribune's annual All-Star Football Game, Arch
had focused national attention on the professional sport.
For more than ten years, Arch had been filling Soldier
Field each August with 100,000 people to see the college
stars play the NFL champion of the previous year. I had
the honor of being head coach of the All-Stars in 1939
and even though we lost to the New York Giants, a great
squad with a fine coach, Steve Owen, it still remains as a
high point in my coaching career as I'm sure it was a high
point for the players.

Arch Ward was a natural born promoter. He had a nose
for what the public wanted and through him, the *Tribune*
became the most sports promotion conscious newspaper
in the country. Now Arch was of the impression that professional football should expand. The NFL owners, many
of whom were yet to make a decent profit out of years of
dedicated effort, were not laboring under the same impression. The few efforts made at expansion during the
war in Boston and Brooklyn had ended in disaster. The
Cleveland franchise, about to win its first league title in
1945, then moved out for the lusher grounds of Los Angeles. Behind this move was the fact that Cleveland
played its home games in League Park, a real cracker box
of a stadium. I tried to convince the Rams to play in

Cleveland Stadium, but Chilli Walsh, the general manager, told me he'd rather turn people away than play to a vast arena of empty seats. He did move the championship game to the Stadium and drew 32,000 fans in bitter, freezing cold. When Bill Veeck took over the Cleveland Indians' baseball club, his first move was away from League Park and into the Stadium, where, in 1946, the newly-founded Cleveland Browns of the All-America Conference began filling the place regularly.

In his quest for a second league, Arch managed to round up several moneyed men who were willing to bet that the country was now ready for two pro leagues. The night before the 1945 All-Star Game, Arch was busy getting ready to announce his new league while others of us enjoyed his hospitality at the *Tribune*'s annual pre-game smoker. George Strickler got wind of what was happening and suggested I ready a statement for the press.

As I recall it, I reminded George that over the years there always had been talk about new professional leagues sprouting up and that as far as I was concerned the All-America Conference should "first get a ball, then make a schedule and then play a game." That roughly was the statement I later gave to the press, but the writers seemed to overlook all but the first phrase, the part about "First get a ball." The new league chose Jimmy Crowley as its commissioner and Jimmy is no guy to try matching witticisms with. The first time we came together, afterwards, for a Quarterback Club luncheon, Jimmy arrived with a football under his arm, saying, "Look, we have a football."

It turned out that the All-America Conference became no joking matter for NFL owners. It became serious com-

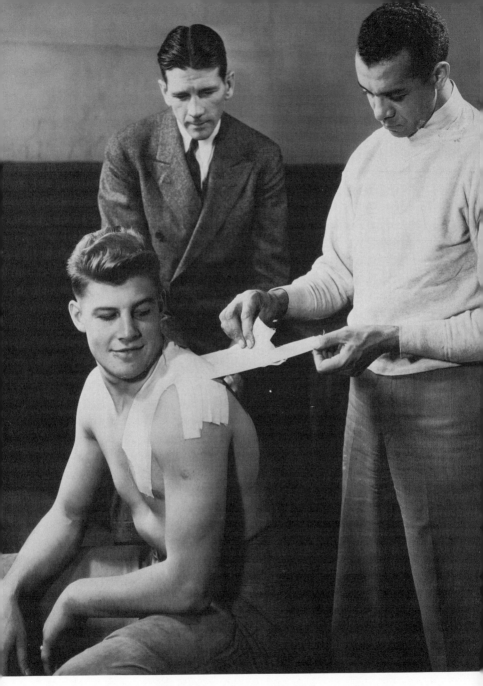

Brue Jackson tapes the shoulder of Vic Vidoni, one of our Duquesne players, while I watch. This picture was used to promote a new fluid that was
applied to the players, so that the tape would come off easily.

Joe E. Brown, while in Pittsburgh attended one of our Duquesne games. With him, from left, are John Harris, who became a promoter of ice shows, Mrs. Harris and Mrs. Brown. I'm the guy with his hat off.

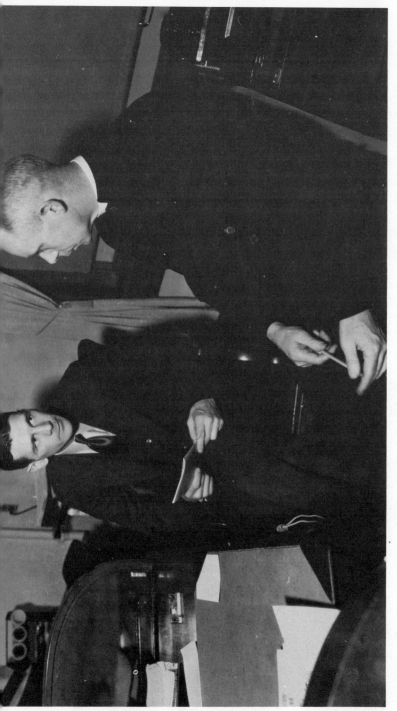

The greatest boss I ever had as a coach, Father John O'Hara of Notre Dame, the first Holy Cross priest to become a cardinal. I may be holding his new book of rules for me.

This was a coast to coast broadcast marking the 25th anniversary of the Army-Notre Dame game in 1938. From left: Louis Merrilatt of the 1913 Army team; me; NBC's Graham McNamee; Gen. Jay Benedict, commandant of West Point; Father O'Hara; Christy Walsh, a promoter close to the Notre Dame scene; Bill Wood, Army's coach, and Elmer Oliphant, one of the Army's greatest football players (class of 1916).

Christy Walsh, second from left, promoted the All American Board of Football. From left, me, Christy, Pop Warner, Howard Jones, and Frank Thomas, a Notre Dame alumnus who coached Alabama into Rose Bowl fame.

The real Knute Rockne is the bust in the middle. The fellow at right is Pat O'Brien, made up for his role as Rock in the 1940 movie, "Knute Rockne, All American."

As Notre Dame's athletic director, I greeted all the luminaries of sport, such as Jack Dempsey, visiting our campus.

The day I received my certificate as a member of College Football's Hall of Fame. From left: Father Edmund Joyce, executive vice president of Notre Dame; Arch Ward of the *Tribune*; Mrs. Rockne with Rock's certificate; the sister of George Gipp; Moose Krause, Notre Dame's athletic director, and me.

(Courtesy *Chicago Tribune*)

petition both at the box office and for professional football talent. And while many owners of Conference teams lost a lot of money, the NFL also spent a lot of money before it pulled off a merger in 1949. Cleveland, Baltimore and San Francisco, the healthiest members of the AAC, merged with the NFL. This set up a very interesting situation in 1950 when the Cleveland Browns defeated the former Cleveland franchise, now the Los Angeles Rams, for the league championship.

CHAPTER EIGHTEEN

All of us have our pet phrases that we have fallen into saying. One of mine has been, "Go quietly." When someone says goodbye to me as they are leaving a table or a party or a meeting, I have fallen into the habit of responding, "Go quietly." Or when I'm the person departing a group, I will say, "I'm going to go quietly." I bring up this habit of speech because I think it perfectly describes how I left football in general, and the National Football League in particular; I went quietly.

Early in January 1946, the NFL had a regular meeting scheduled in the Commodore Hotel in New York, a place where I still stay when I go to the big city, and the hotel where I always held our league meetings. I was asleep the night before the meeting when I heard a knocking on my door and opened it to find George Strickler and Jimmy Conzelman. Jimmy, who was coaching the Cardinals, and

George reported that a group of owners had just completed a rump meeting and had voted not to renew my contract, which expired in about a month. Later on, after Jimmy had gone, one of the other owners also came by with the same message.

The next morning I went to the meeting room that had been set aside for us to open the proceedings. I soon found that I was banging a gavel to an empty room. Later, a delegation of owners came to my room and politely confirmed the reports of the night before: my contract would not be renewed; however, I would be kept on the payroll for a year as a consultant. I thanked them for this gesture of generosity, but politely declined the consulting arrangement.

Years later, Tim Mara of the Giants liked to tell how he had originally opposed my selection as commissioner, but after the others had voted for me, he said he would be my biggest backer when the chips were down. Tim said he was behind having the owners agree to the one year consulting deal. He may well have been the man responsible for this offer; which I did not feel I should accept.

In short, I was ready to "go quietly."

After leaving, I tried to make it a point to keep to myself any feelings I might have about the professional game and how it was being operated. Then, in 1949, Vincent X. Flaherty, the columnist for the *Los Angeles Examiner*, cornered me at a party the night before a Notre Dame-Southern California game, where the 1924 team was going to be honored on its 25th Anniversary. Pro football was just completing its fourth year of two-league competition, and Flaherty asked me what I thought about the situation.

I told him I thought the NFL should have recognized the All-America Conference after one season; that two leagues were good for the sport, but only if they got together. I recalled one of my first meetings with Judge Landis where he advised me that the future of pro football depended on development of two leagues. The judge drew on his long experience of trust-busting and cautioned me to the effect that "where there is one league, a monopoly, the owners will try to run the show to suit themselves." How right he turned out to be!

How often we had sat through the night while one owner harangued all the others over his dissatisfaction with a rule change or some provision in the league constitution.

And then, when a second league did form and did survive its first season, the senior league continued to battle it tooth and nail at a high cost to itself.

A few weeks after my expounding to Flaherty on the need for the two leagues to get together, they did make peace. But only one league resulted, and that's how things stood until the American Football League came along a decade later. By now a younger, yet wiser man, or so it seemed to me, was in the commissioner's chair—Pete Rozelle. The owners, who had done battle again until the new league began bidding up the price of players way beyond what pro football people ever dreamed could happen, came to terms. Wisely, a peace pact was arranged, and today practically every team in both leagues is making it both at the box office and on the balance sheet. The Super Bowl game has attained a status among football fans that the World Series enjoys among baseball fans.

The New York Jets' surprising victory in the 1969 game gave this new event even added glamour. The American League at last had come into its own and had proven that it could play the best the NFL had to offer and beat them.

I have read that Pete Rozelle forecasts a bright future for both leagues, and I could not agree with him more. Nor could I think of any single man who deserves greater praise for making this possible than Pete.

"And he's such a young man," one of my friends remarked. To which I replied, "Well, how old do you think I was when I was commissioner?" My friend thought a minute and then said, "Well I guess you couldn't have been too old yourself since that goes back a few years."

Actually I was thirty-seven when I started; forty-two when I finished.

The job has its hard side, but it also has its fun side. And probably the most fun I can recall was going to the White House in 1945 to present a gold pass to league games to the President of the United States. Baseball had been doing this for years and we had decided it was time for football to get into the act.

George Marshall, who owned the Washington home team, accompanied me to the White House, whose occupant was Harry S Truman.

He received us most graciously in his office and, as group spokesman, I thanked him for taking time away from a busy day to let us get some publicity for our sport. "Think nothing of it," Mr. Truman told us.

Then, pointing to his desk which was covered with

piles of papers and documents, I said, "But you certainly seem to have a lot of work to deal with."

"Well," Mr. Truman replied, "I read through each pile of papers and make up my mind and then push it aside and move on to the next pile."

On the desk, I recall, was a sign that stated, "The Buck-Passing Stops Here."

It seemed like a fine sign for the office of our President and one worth having on your desk, too, if you happened to be commissioner of football.

CHAPTER NINETEEN

At forty-two my football career was over; I had spent six-teen years as a coach, five as a commissioner, and many as a player. Now, of course, I had to find another job, and I came to the conclusion that my next job would not be in sports.

I was approached with one sports offer, to become ath-letic director for a new college in the Southwest, which since has grown to considerable prominence. Without hesitation, I declined it gratefully. From now on, I was going to be up in the stands and cheering as the winners went by. I needed a change, and all my years in football made a change to the business world quite easy. I had been able to travel across the land and meet hundreds of people, many of them businessmen. My football jobs in the last twenty years, as an athletic director and the head of a professional league, had exposed me to the dollars and cents side of the sport. I also had to learn how to get up on my feet and make an after-dinner speech. I possessed some of the equipment for a new career.

Shortly after cleaning up loose ends at the NFL office, an old friend, Tom Delanty, steered me to Shippers Car Line, the freight car leasing subsidiary of ACF Industries. There I became assistant to the president, Bob Rogers, and worked in sales with Art Williams, then a vice-president of the company and later president of Stanray in Chicago. This introduced me to an industry in which I have spent the remainder of my full-time working years.

After two years with Shippers, I was lured away to the largest company in freight car leasing, General American Transportation Corporation, by two of the finest businessmen I have ever had the privilege of working for: Lester Selig and Sam Laud. Lester was a sales genius; Sam a financial genius and together they built GATX into one of the country's most formidable transportation companies. In May, 1968, I reached age sixty-five and was retired from GATX after twenty years of truly happy association with hundreds of men in our nation's transportation industry—men who sell transportation services and men who buy them.

As part of the GATX sales organization, I continued to have the opportunity for travel around the country and the chance to give occasional speeches about the good old days of football as I remembered them. I also was able to keep in contact with the many friends I had made during the years I was part of the sport.

No book is big enough to list all of the names of the people who made these times so much fun.

First of all, there are the sportswriters. I've mentioned some of them, yet nowhere near the number that I knew, beginning with Johnny O'Donnell in Davenport, Iowa; Al Abrams, Charles J. Doyle and Les Biederman in Pittsburgh; and the late Jim Costin in South Bend. Jim always complained that I didn't give him any breaks on our Notre Dame team even though he was a home town sports editor.

"But, Jim," I'd say, "I tell you everything I know." "Yeah, but you won't let me print it," he'd reply.

The Eastern writers always were kind to us: Bill Corum, Frank Graham, Stanley Woodward, Red Smith, Arthur Daley, Damon Runyon, Jimmy Powers, Dan Parker, and not to forget the dean of them all while he was alive, Granny Rice.

Until Granny died, I tried never to miss the party given each year at the Racquet Club in Philadelphia the night before the Army-Navy game. Granny would hold forth with an eloquence unmatched as he recounted the great moments in the golden age of sports.

Looking over the home town papers in Chicago, I see very few bylines of old friends remaining. George Strickler, Leo Fischer and John Carmichael are still at it, but Warren Brown and Wilfrid Smith have retired, Arch Ward and Ed Burns are dead and Jim Kearns has moved into public relations.

Another group I can't forget are those Notre Dame alumni who were so helpful to me over the years: I. A. O'Shaughnessy of St. Paul; Doctor Maurice Keady, who hosted our teams so often before Army games at the Westchester Biltmore; Joe Byrne of the N.Y. Port Authority and his father before him; Frank Walker, the former postmaster general; Tom O'Neill of General Tire, and, of course, Doc O'Donnell. Two of this group I still see whenever I can: Judge Roger Kiley and Joe LaFortune.

Joe is in the oil business in Tulsa and has been a great benefactor of his alma mater. When he was in town last, he tried to sign me up as his personal recruiter for Notre Dame, to get them some good boys from the Chicago area. I suggested a younger man might do better in light of what I read about the generation gap.

Rog Kiley was an All-American end at Notre Dame the first year I made the team. He was one of my staunchest backers when I became the coach there. He even had me formally introduced to Chicago's City Council, and the picture of that event still gives me chuckles seeing all of the politicians trying to elbow into the picture with Roger, then-Mayor Ed Kelly, and myself.

Finally, there are the players, the ones I played with and the ones who played for me.

Only six of us are now left from the starting team of that 1924 squad that became Four Horsemen and Seven Mules. Last December, I traveled to New York to see the team captain, Adam Walsh, inducted into the National Collegiate Football Hall of Fame. Adam, Rip Miller, and Chuck Collins are the linemen still with us. Now that Harry is gone, Don Miller, Jim Crowley and I don't get together as often as we should, and we are what is left of the backfield.

From time to time, I hear from one or the other of the players I coached. I'm a poor correspondent and usually take ages to write back. I make a point of attending the

Chicago Tribune's annual smoker before its All-Star game because I see quite a few of the Notre Dame boys who live in the Chicago area at that affair.

A real joy is running into an old-timer whom you played against. This happened recently when Ernie Nevers was in Chicago and stopped off at the Chicago Athletic Club for lunch. They had to pry us apart so Ernie could catch his plane home. I recall one thing we discussed. "Ernie," I said, "I never ran into a dirty football player when I was playing." "No, Elmer, I didn't either," he replied.

Both of us would like to think the same is true today. Football is a great sport, a lot of fun for boys of every age, and it should be kept that way. It's a sport, always was, and always should be.